SECRET
BEND, OREGON

A Guide to the Weird, Wonderful, and Obscure

Joshua Savage

REEDY PRESS

Reedy Press
PO Box 5131
St. Louis, MO 63139
reedypress.com

Library of Congress Control Number: 2024939292
ISBN: 9781681065588

Design by Jill Halpin

Unless otherwise indicated, all photos are courtesy of the author or in the public domain.

We (the publisher and the author) have done our best to provide the most accurate information available when this book was completed. However, we make no warranty, guarantee, or promise about the accuracy, completeness, or currency of the information provided, and we expressly disclaim all warranties, express or implied. Please note that attractions, company names, addresses, websites, and phone numbers are subject to change or closure, and this is outside of our control. We are not responsible for any loss, damage, injury, or inconvenience that may occur due to the use of this book. When exploring new destinations, please do your homework before you go. You are responsible for your own safety and health when using this book.

Printed in the United States of America
24 25 26 27 28   5 4 3 2 1

As always, I dedicate this book to my wife, Niki,
and my daughters, Sofi and Kaia. They make this journey of life
and travel so much more meaningful and exciting.

Green Lakes Trail

CONTENTS

Hatfield Ponds

INTRODUCTION

Central Oregon possesses a fascinating history. We often hear popular tales of Indigenous people, fur trappers, sheepherders, cattlemen, homesteaders, railroads, lumber mills, and, most recently, recreation. The lesser-known but equally intriguing stories talk of ghost towns, mining, moonshine, cults, and everything in between.

In popularity, Bend is the hub of the area, yet much more exists in the High Desert region. While writing *100 Things to Do in Bend, Oregon, Before You Die*, I became more enamored with the area and wanted to dig deeper into its history and uniqueness. Too often we overlook these interesting stories in favor of a delicious IPA, a new food truck, or a trip to REI to get the latest gear, always hunting for the next best thing. Yet, I think it's just as important to learn about the rich past and the smaller things that make a place distinctive.

My goal with *Secret Bend, Oregon* is to present a good mix of past and present sprinkled with education and entertainment. Hopefully, readers will develop a deeper appreciation for the lesser-known aspects of the High Desert. This book encompasses much of Deschutes and other counties in Central Oregon, but of course it cannot begin to cover every part of the region.

Writing such a book has been rewarding and fun. During my research, I learned a ton about the state's history and culture. If I can pass down or preserve some of the stories and eccentricities of the area, then my time and effort was worth every second.

As amazing as Bend is, if you are only exploring the one city, you are missing out. Branch out and explore!

Join the journey to explore and learn about Central Oregon by visiting my Facebook group @100+ThingstoDoinBend, or read my column "Savage in Bend" in the local *Source Weekly* newspaper.

THE BEGINNING

Where did it all (Bend) begin?

Every area has a history, so why not start where it all began? Many locals claim Farewell Bend as one of their favorite public parks, and its name originates from where the town first started. In 1877, pioneer and entrepreneur John Y. Todd set up his Farewell Bend Ranch on the east side of the Deschutes River in what is now the Old Mill District. Sources say he purchased this piece of prime land for only $60 and a couple of saddle horses! Many travelers attempted to ford (cross) the river in this area, and it soon became an established stopping point. Financial difficulties eventually forced Todd to sell the land to John Sisemore, who set up a post office. The postal authorities thought Farewell Bend was too long a name and dropped the "Farewell." On January 4, 1905, the small town of Bend became incorporated and has been growing ever since!

These days the reasons for the popularity of the Farewell Bend Park are many. Runners and hikers have easy access to the Deschutes River Trail. A small beach serves as an entry point to the river for swimming or floating. A paved path through the park offers

FAREWELL BEND

WHAT: Farewell Bend Park

WHERE: 1000 SW Reed Market Rd.

COST: Free

PRO TIP: Get there early to get a parking spot.

Check out Greg Congleton's *Two Bits* horse sculpture near the bridge. Made from recycled materials including a sewing machine, rakes, wrenches, and other random recycled pieces, it's an unbelievably cool ode to Bend's logging history.

Located right on the Deschutes River, Farewell Bend Park is a favorite among locals and visitors.

amazing views of the river, and signposts provide info about the city's history. Twenty-two acres of well-maintained green space provide plenty of room for frisbee throwing, a lumber-themed playground for the kids, a pavilion for picnics, and countless other outside activities. John would be amazed to see the many changes!

A VOLCANO HERE IN THE CITY?!

What do you mean there is a volcano in the middle of the city?!

Yep, Pilot Butte, the popular tourist spot and landmark that locals see every day, is a volcano. Bend and three other cities in the United States have one INSIDE their city limits! No worries, though; this one is extinct.

Long before the first settlers arrived in Bend, this volcanic cinder cone already had been etched on the area's landscape for many thousands of years. Indigenous people used it as a way to track wildlife during the summer. Later, fur trappers, homesteaders with big dreams, and other travelers used it as a beacon to locate routes and where to cross on the Deschutes River.

Red Butte, Pilot Knob—it has gone through a few names. Then along came Thomas Clark, a fellow who led a group of the first European settlers who camped on the future site of Bend. When he called it Pilot Butte, the name stuck.

The 480-foot summit is open year-round to visitors. During the warmer months of the year the state park's gates are open, and vehicles can drive to the top. In winter the gates close, but a hike to the top still offers an amazing panoramic view of Bend.

In case you wanted to know the other cities with volcanoes inside their city limits:
- Mount Tabor in Portland, Oregon
- Diamond Head in Honolulu, Hawaii
- Mount Jackson in Jackson, Mississippi (Who would have guessed Mississippi?!)

The view from atop Pilot Butte

BUTTE WITH A VIEW

WHAT: Pilot Butte State Park

WHERE: 1310 NE Hwy. 20

COST: Free

PRO TIP: A hike up is more fun than driving!

The peaks of Mount Bachelor, the Three Sisters, Mount Jefferson, and even Oregon's highest peak, Mount Hood, are visible on a clear, sunny day. No need to worry about eruptions any time soon, but catching a sunset from atop a volcano is pretty magical.

QUITE THE CHARACTER

Who was this Klondike Kate gal I've heard about?

Once upon a time a lady named Kathleen Eloisa Rockwell rode into Central Oregon with a big plume hat, a glittering dancehall gown, and flashy jewelry. As you can imagine, she quickly became the talk of the town. Better known as Klondike Kate, she was a well-known vaudeville dancer in bigger cities like Spokane and Vancouver, but when heartbreak and scandal threatened her career, she decided to leave the fame behind and set up a homestead near Brothers, Oregon.

She always maintained her colorful character, and locals would see her working the land while still wearing her bright silk gowns and jewelry. A charmer, she loved to entertain guests and was a first-class storyteller. Gossip often surrounded Kate, and they say many wives worried about her overzealous friendliness.

After Kate came to Bend in 1917, she fell in love with the area and became part of it.

Her generous spirit fed the hungry, tended the sick during the influenza epidemic, and even counseled young ladies about love affairs. Whether or not you admired Aunt Kate, she had a huge influence on Bend during her lifetime.

The Queen of the Yukon was also known as one of the first rockhounders. They say she drove her battered car through the

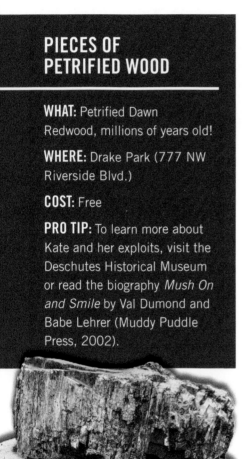

PIECES OF PETRIFIED WOOD

WHAT: Petrified Dawn Redwood, millions of years old!

WHERE: Drake Park (777 NW Riverside Blvd.)

COST: Free

PRO TIP: To learn more about Kate and her exploits, visit the Deschutes Historical Museum or read the biography *Mush On and Smile* by Val Dumond and Babe Lehrer (Muddy Puddle Press, 2002).

Kate's petrified wood at Drake Park

desert collecting thundereggs, jasper, and every other semiprecious stone she could find. Her collection was used to eventually build a massive fireplace in her Franklin Avenue home. Today, a plaque is in the location of the original house. A few of Kate's possessions (like her shiny silver shoes) are on display at the Deschutes Historical Museum.

In Drake Park sit two large, petrified stumps from Dawn Redwood, a tree that was supposedly prominent in Oregon around 30 million years ago! These were found on Kate's homestead in Brothers, ensuring that she will be remembered for ages to come.

A PHOENIX FROM THE ASHES

What's the story behind this O'Kane fella I keep hearing about?

Destroyed by fire not once but twice, the O'Kane Building downtown is like a phoenix that rises from the ashes.

Hugh O'Kane was an Irish immigrant who ended up in Bend in 1904. After gallivanting around the country as a tailor, sailor, boxer, smuggler, gambler, and other questionable occupations, his first endeavor on the corner of Oregon Street and Bond was a saloon. The infamous Bend fire of 1905 ravaged it, but on the bright side, the city promptly created its first fire-protection system afterward. O'Kane quickly rebuilt in the same spot and opened a hotel. Ten years later, that burned down as well!

Determined not to be beaten, he immediately rebuilt again in 1916, this time a grander structure with reinforced concrete to protect against future flames. O'Kane added decorative green tiles, hand-

DOWNTOWN'S LARGEST AND MOST RESILIENT BUILDING

WHAT: The O'Kane Building

WHERE: 115 NW Oregon Ave.

COST: Free

PRO TIP: Take some time to really explore this unique building. Admire the intricate designs and stained glass, the Bend logo, and some of the unique local businesses inside the building.

The *Amazing Life of Hugh O'Kane* is a piece of artwork that depicts some of the many exploits of the daring Irishman. Find it at the building named after him at McMenamins.

carved wooden doorframes, and stained glass windows that feature the Bend emblem that became the popular city symbol we use today. A theater, apartments, and offices originally filled the huge space. When Deschutes became its own county and broke away from Crook, the building was used temporarily as the county's first courthouse.

Today, over 100 years later, the historic building still boasts the title of the largest commercial structure in downtown Bend and is home to several thriving businesses. Thanks to a lesson in determination by Hugh O'Kane, it contains one of the richest histories in the city.

Views of the O'Kane Building and the famous Bend logo.

KEEPERS OF HISTORY

Where is the best spot to learn about the history of Central Oregon?

The best place to get schooled on Central Oregon history is hands-down the Deschutes Historical Museum. A repository of knowledge for the area, the imposing Richardsonian Romanesque building hosts a wealth of information about the early days of Bend, the importance of the forests and the mills of the area, homesteading, the famed Bend Water Pageant, snow skiing, the effects of the 1918 Spanish influenza and the more recent pandemic, astronauts training in the Lava Lands, and other endlessly intriguing information.

What now houses the museum once held studious children of all grades. The Reid School, as it was once known, was named for Ruth Reid. Most of her prodigious life was spent in education, first as a teacher and then as the first principal of Bend. A replica of Ms. Reid's classroom is in the upstairs portion of the building. If you dare, attempt to answer the "Questions for the 8th Grade Diploma," quite challenging even for a present-day adult!

DESCHUTES HISTORY

WHAT: The Reid School (Deschutes Historical Museum)

WHERE: 129 NW Idaho Ave.

COST: $5, free for members

PRO TIP: The Deschutes County Public Library often has free passes to the museum. Check the library website or ask while there.

Consider becoming a member and supporting the museum. For only $25 annually, you can help preserve the past!

The Deschutes Historical Museum also reaches beyond the building to educate the community. A downloadable phone app has a Cruisin' 97 feature that highlights significant places around the area. The museum hosts History Pubs throughout the year, super cool night markets during the summer, and many other fun events like the Chili Feed, the Little Woody, and Haunting Tours. The museum is a true steward of the past, and Central Oregon is lucky to have such a place!

The Deschutes Historical Museum, once upon a time the Reid School

THE MCKAY COTTAGE

Who is this McKay guy?

From time to time, we might see names around town and wonder about their origin. For example, after floating the Deschutes, folks usually get out near McKay Park. We might drive down McKay Avenue to get to the river. Most importantly, we know the popular McKay Cottage for a delicious breakfast or lunch, an early morning mimosa or Bloody Mary, and sitting around warm firepits with blankets on a chilly day.

Once upon a time the home that is now Bend's favorite breakfast place was owned by Clyde and Olive McKay. Clyde was an outdoorsman and local Bend legend. After arriving in Bend in the early 1900s, he played a large role in the development of the town. His business, the Bend Company, became the first sawmill near the Deschutes River and helped lure larger mills like Shevlin Hixon and Brooks-Scanlon to the area.

Get more than a tasty breakfast at McKay Cottage.

McKay Cottage Restaurant

Later he dabbled in politics as the county's first treasurer, served as a member of the city council and school board, and was a member of many local civic clubs. Clyde eventually became an Oregon game warden who helped stock the local lakes with fish and created the area's first hatchery.

Built in 1916, the McKay Cottage originally sat on Mirror Pond. It was moved to its current location in 1973 and restored to its former glory. So next time you're drinking a tasty beverage at McKay Cottage, raise your glass and toast Clyde for helping make Bend what it is today!

Clyde McKay and other notable Bendites are buried at Pilot Butte Cemetery, a cemetery with headstones dating back to 1903—older than the city itself!

BEND'S OLDEST BUILDING

What is the oldest building in Bend?

The Goodwillie-Allen-Rademacher House, aka the Commons Cafe, sits downtown overlooking Mirror Pond. The home boasts the distinction of being Bend's oldest structure and the second-oldest craftsman-style bungalow in Oregon.

COMMONS CAFE AND TAPROOM

WHAT: The oldest structure in Bend (Goodwillie-Allen-Rademacher House)

WHERE: 875 NW Brooks St.

COST: Free to view, but grab a reasonably priced beverage or snack to enjoy.

PRO TIP: Try one of the seasonal drink specials at the Commons Cafe and then chill outside and people-watch.

Arthur L. Goodwillie constructed the home in 1904. An influential Bendite, he became the first mayor of Bend but eventually returned to his hometown of Chicago. He sold the house to Herbert and Alice Allen, another prominent couple, who lived there for over 20 years. Thus, the name Goodwillie-Allen. When Herbert passed away, the home was bought by the esteemed physician Dr. Clyde Rademacher. He and his wife lived there until they both died in the 1980s, the longest-tenured of all the residents.

Afterward the bungalow sat vacant for a while. In fact, it was almost razed to build a parking lot! Fortunately, a forward-thinking community group saw the benefit of preserving it.

During spring and summer, stroll by Libby's Garden at the Commons Cafe to see all sorts of native plants popping with color.

14

Summer blooms at Commons Cafe and Taproom.

Better known as the Commons Cafe these days, the building hosts live music, open-mic nights, and other events. Outside, the Commons Plaza is a popular spot for many downtown happenings—races, a Christmas tree lighting, Halloween costume contests, and much more. Whether people-watching or enjoying a beverage in the area, we are all adding to the history of Bend whenever we visit.

SMOKESTACKS ON THE HORIZON

Why are there three large smokestacks in the middle of an outdoor mall?

Once upon a time, not so long ago, the waters of the Deschutes River were teeming with large logs of pine. Pond Monkeys, as they were known, would jump from log to log attempting to guide them into the intake for the sawmill. Smoke from the mills filled the air, and you had better be careful not to step on rebar when walking in the area. The Central Oregon landscape was dominated by the timber industry.

Today, the water looks clean and the air feels pure. Rather than the smell of burning wood, we might get a more agreeable whiff of hops from the nearby Deschutes Brewery. While shopping and dining in a modern outdoor mall or practicing fly casting, it might be easy to forget the mills of old. Well, except for the three large smokestacks towering over 200 feet above us.

Once housed atop the Brooks-Scanlon Mill powerhouse building, the smokestacks are now part of the

THE OLD MILL DISTRICT

WHAT: Towering smokestacks

WHERE: The REI building in the Old Mill District (380 SW Powerhouse Dr.)

COST: Free to explore, unless you decide to shop

PRO TIP: Check out the art all around the Old Mill. From dragons and colorful stairs to the must-take selfie of the Bend, Oregon, mural, the area is full of colorful and unique works!

Bend's Old Mill District was featured in the HBO documentary *Our Towns* as an example of the potential of cities to remake themselves and reenergize their economies.

well-known outdoor company REI. Other historical buildings in the area, 11 in fact, also remind us of the once-mighty mills that powered the economy. For example, DeWilde Art Glass used to be the home of a structure called the Little Red Shed, where the mills' fire trucks were stored. Cylindrical cement footings in front of Tumalo Creek Kayak & Rental once used as burners are now host to brightly colored flowers during warmer months.

The mills are an integral part of Oregon's history. When Bend had to pivot to economically survive, the incorporation of past and present to create the Old Mill District was a brilliant idea. It shows we can change with the times while respecting those who came before us.

Bend's iconic smokestacks above REI

THE BOX FACTORY

Why do they call it the Box Factory?

The Box Factory is a favorite hangout spot among Bendites, but this wasn't always the case. The popular destination was once part of the mighty Brooks-Scanlon empire. Built in 1916 when the mills were ubiquitous, box factories were places where the leftover scraps of wood were saved. Rather than wasting them, they made good use of the leftovers and turned them into items such as pencils and boxes to store things like fruit, soap, milk, and even ammunition. Quite the recyclers, eh?

The mills closed in the 1980s, and not long afterward, the building was set for demolition. Yet again, some creative and forward-thinking individuals decided to refurbish the original structure and maintain its history. A major project indeed, and another amazing example of how Bend preserves and respects its past. The original cupola has been maintained as the iconic mark of a mill building, and much of the woodwork and columns were preserved. The restoration was completed in 2016, just in time to celebrate the building's centennial!

After the Box Factory's success, the area around it has blossomed. A hotel, the Crosscut Warming Hut, food trucks, and the huge mixed-use area being developed—Jackstraw—are sure to make this an even bigger hot spot for locals and tourists!

Front entrance to the many places to explore in the Box Factory.

Today, the Box Factory has over 35 local merchants with amazingly diverse services ranging from food and drink to home furnishings and outdoor supplies. The list is too long to name them all, but this is a special part of town, a small village of its own, and one worth frequenting often.

THE LONE WOOD BUILDING

Why does downtown have one lone wooden building while the others are all brick?

Walking along Wall Street, passersby may or may not notice the odd store out among the brick buildings. It appears to fit in perfectly, but take a closer look and the N.P Smith Hardware Building stands out from the rest as the only remaining wood structure in downtown Bend.

Nicolas Smith was an enterprising young man. In 1909 he built the hardware store with an apartment upstairs for his family. His shop sold household goods like butter churns and stoves and also provided supplies for hunters and fishermen. Rumor has it that he was the first to sell gasoline to the motorists when automobiles came to Bend. Basically, if he thought something would sell, he stocked it. Nicolas retired from the hardware business in 1930, but the building continued to host other businesses, and his daughter actually lived in the apartment upstairs until the 1980s.

Downtown Bend has a history of fires, like those that burnt down the O'Kane Building twice. Miraculously, while most others were damaged or completely destroyed, Smith's Hardware survived and still stands strong. In 1984 the building was added to the National Register of Historical Places. A placard on the outside wall attests to its unique history.

One of downtown's most unique gift shops, Lone Crow Bungalow, now occupies the downstairs, while the upstairs remains a residence.

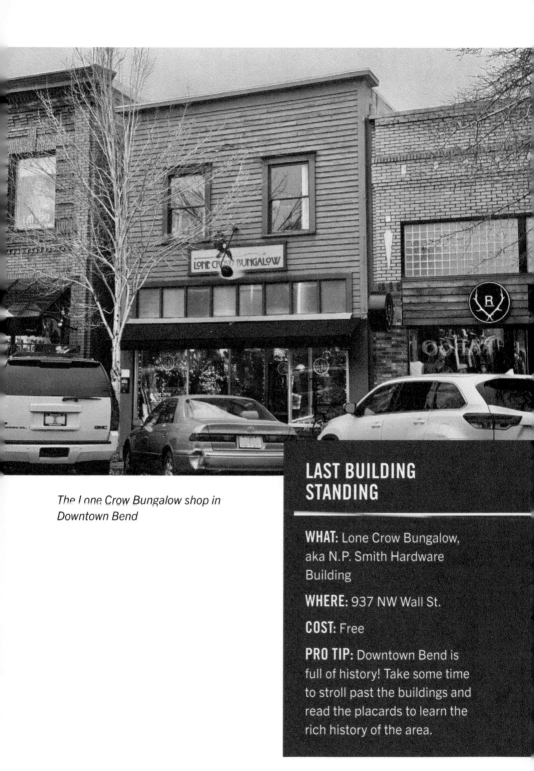

The Lone Crow Bungalow shop in Downtown Bend

LAST BUILDING STANDING

WHAT: Lone Crow Bungalow, aka N.P. Smith Hardware Building

WHERE: 937 NW Wall St.

COST: Free

PRO TIP: Downtown Bend is full of history! Take some time to stroll past the buildings and read the placards to learn the rich history of the area.

SCHOOL ON THE RIVER

How cool would it be to have school near the river?

Imagine learning math or English while you hear the Deschutes River flowing peacefully in the background. During break or lunch, you walk along the bank, watch the wildlife, or play near the water, maybe even take a dip. Well, the first kids who went to school in Bend got to do just that!

Today's Drake Park was once home to Bend's very first schoolhouse. In 1887, before Bend was even a town, a log cabin was built near the bank of the river. Not more than a few hundred square feet, the structure housed all grade levels. It also served as storage for fur trappers, as a community center, and as a Sunday school. Understandably, the cabin became too small to house the growing number of students (over 200 by 1905), and a bond was issued to build a new six-room school (the Reid School).

Later, the wood cabin became home to the *Bend Bulletin*, the well-known local paper that is still in circulation today. Though the original log cabin was torn down

TIME FOR CLASS

WHAT: Bend's first schoolhouse

WHERE: Pilot Butte Middle School (a replica) at 1501 NE Neff Rd.

COST: Free

PRO TIP: Stop by Pilot Butte Middle School when school is not in session to take a look at the log cabin. It will amaze you that such a small structure served so many useful purposes!

Bend-La Pine School District currently has over 18,400 students. No way would they fit in the wood cabin!

A replica of the original schoolhouse can be seen at Pilot Butte Middle School.

long ago, a replica sits on the property of Pilot Butte Middle School. Seeing it is a stark reminder of how far we have come in terms of growth and development. It also proves that an education can be had anywhere.

BEND'S LIVING ROOM

Which iconic location is known as "Bend's living room?"

The neon marquee of the Tower Theatre lights up the downtown streets of Bend at night. Meanwhile, the crowds inside are entertained year-round with movies, concerts, comedy, and other live performances. Yet, the venue has fallen on some tough times in the past and has not always been such a lively, dynamic spot.

The current structure was built in just over 90 days in a popular emerging architectural style known as streamline moderne. In 1940, Tower Theatre opened with its first film, *Four Wives*, and for over 40 years the venue provided exciting entertainment for the citizens of Bend.

Like the rest of Central Oregon, the theatre fell on tough times when the mills closed. TV and drive-in theatres also caused attendance to drop significantly. Neglected and outdated, the Tower fell into disrepair and finally closed its doors in 1993.

However, as we have already learned about Bendites and historic structures, it didn't take long for a community-based nonprofit group to raise money to restore the cherished institution. In 2004, the newly refurbished and upgraded

POWER OF THE TOWER

WHAT: The Tower Theatre

WHERE: 835 NW Wall St.

COST: Free to view, events vary

PRO TIP: Theatre goers get a much more intimate feeling when watching live performances. Be sure to check some out!

Before the Tower was built, the space housed a bakery owned by Maren Gribskov and Eleanor Bechen, the same entrepreneurial ladies who went on to open another well-known Bend destination, the Pine Tavern!

The book displayed on the marqee at the Tower Theatre looks familiar! A best seller?

Tower Theatre reopened and reemerged as one of the town's most iconic spots. Except for a brief closure during the COVID pandemic (like almost every place), the venue has thrived and is often referred to as "Bend's Living Room."

RAILROAD BATTLES

Why is there a train depot in the Old Mill District but no tracks?

As was true with many cities across the United States, trains were a significant influence in Bend's growth. The race to bring the railroad to Bend—known as "Harriman versus Hill" or "Wall Street's Great Railroad War"—is quite a fascinating story.

Two wealthy individuals, Edward H. Harriman of Union Pacific and James H. Hill of the Great Northern Railroad, both wanted to be the first to bring tracks to Central Oregon no matter what the cost. They literally battled through the Deschutes River Canyon in order to connect Bend to the rest of the country. Ultimately, they wanted to open the markets from the east of the United States to the west in California.

Workers laid tracks on each side of the Deschutes River at a record pace, and rumor has it that hand-to-hand fights between the two sides often broke out. Large boulders were rolled down steep hills to block paths, supplies were sabotaged, and sharpshooters were supposedly hired to deter violence. Hill became the winner when tracks finally reached Bend in 1911. The town became the terminus of the Oregon Trunkline for two decades.

The train depot located near
Hayden Homes Amphitheater

By the 1990s the train depot no longer served a purpose and was in the way of a new route for Hwy. 97. One by one, the stones (about 4,000 of them!) were moved to their current location in the Old Mill District where they served as an art studio run by Bend Parks & Recreation for many years. The former depot is now utilized by Hayden Homes amphitheater and still represents an intriguing part of Bend's historical development.

CHOO CHOO TRAIN

WHAT: Oregon Trunk Railroad Depot

WHERE: Free

COST: 313 Shevlin-Hixon Dr.

PRO TIP: If you're a history buff, the book *Harriman vs Hill. Wall Street's Great Railroad War* by Larry Haeg, University of Minnesota Press, 2013, is a fun read and a fascinating account of the railroad war between these two men.

Another nearby historic train depot is being used in Redmond to serve up every adult's favorite morning beverage (the Redmond Coffee Company).

PILOT BUTTE INN

Where was this Pilot Butte Inn I hear so much about?

Pilot Butte Inn was once the grandest hotel in all of Central Oregon. Prestigious guests from around the country visited, including esteemed first lady Eleanor Roosevelt, actor Humphrey Bogart, and former President Herbert Hoover.

The Swiss chalet-style structure was located overlooking the Deschutes River at the corner of Newport Avenue and Wall Street. Built in 1917, it had three stories consisting mostly of locally sourced materials such as lava rock and pine. The Pilot Butte Inn hosted conventions, weddings, birthday parties, balls, and other large festivities. And although Oregon was a dry state, plenty of spirits somehow made their way to most of these lively events.

Hard times hit in the 1960s, when the inn kept changing owners and maintenance lapsed. Some citizens wanted to preserve this piece of Bend's history, but 1973 brought demolition. Today, there is no indication that the hotel even existed in this location.

However, a unique remnant of the inn remains. A massive stone fireplace inside the building was carefully dismantled stone by stone

PILOT BUTTE INN

WHAT: The fireplace from the original Pilot Butte Inn

WHERE: Bend Athletic Club

COST: Free, but why not get a membership and get in shape?

PRO TIP: Other mementos from the Pilot Butte Inn can be found at Deschutes Historical Museum.

Interested in historic hotels? Wolf Creek Inn, now operated by the Oregon State Park Service, is the oldest in Oregon. It was built in 1883, and guests can still reserve a room. Novelist Jack London stayed there!

The original fireplace from the Pilot Butte Inn is now located at the Bend Athletic Club.

and then reconstructed at the Bend Athletic Club (BAC). One can admire the stonework and imagine warmth in front of the giant fire on a cold winter day. No membership is required to take a peek at this unique piece of Bend's history, but after seeing all the facilities at BAC, you may want to join and keep fit.

SECRET ROOMS

What's so secret about McMenamins?

Though it's hardly a secret these days, a book titled *Secret Bend, Oregon* would not be complete without mentioning the hidden rooms of McMenamins Old St. Francis School.

The St. Francis building was once a bustling Catholic school with children hard at work or playfully roaming the halls. When the school relocated in the year 2000, two brothers from Portland, Mike and Brian McMenamin, purchased the building. As they had with many of their other historical properties, they transformed the school into an eclectic destination with all sorts of onsite activities.

The property now hosts a restaurant, a soaking pool, a movie theater, a cigar room, lodging, and more.

Later, additional buildings were constructed as hotels. One of these, known as the Art House, has some secrets to discover. Besides the artistic concert posters that fill the walls, each of the three floors in this building has one special room, and it's not just for hotel guests. Curious visitors will find a black-light room with surreal designs reminiscent of *Alice in Wonderland* on the first

ENTERTAINING SECRETS

WHAT: McMenamins and its secret rooms

WHERE: 700 NW Bond St.

COST: Free to roam the secret rooms, but the many other attractions here cost money.

PRO TIP: You should really try the Cajun tots. Best ever!

McMenamins has over 60 locations across Washington and Oregon, most of them housed in historical buildings. Grab a passport and visit as many as you can!

A surprise awaits behind the doors of the Broom Closet!

floor. On the second floor, search for a room with chalkboard walls full of aphorisms, autographs, and miscellaneous scribbled art.

Finally, on the third floor, attempt to locate the Broom Closet. Once inside, a speakeasy with the most relaxing, chilled vibe you can imagine awaits. Plus, the drinks are superb. Treat yourself after your magical discoveries.

YAKAYA

Why are all those kayaks hanging in the air?!

Love or hate them, Bend has tons of roundabouts throughout the city, with more being built all the time. Although official protocol exists, it seems no one can agree on the exact etiquette when it comes to driving them. To use or not to use a blinker? Do I make a complete stop or simply yield?

However, one thing most people love about the roundabouts is the distinctive art in the center. Since the early 1970s the Arts in Public Places (AiPP) committee has been responsible for transforming the visual and cultural landscapes of Bend with creative, permanent pieces of art.

Perhaps the most fascinating is *Yakaya*, the sculpture created by Troy Pillow in 2010. This mixture of modern design and nature has nine yellow, blue, orange, and red kayaks that form the shape of flower petals. The stamen is made from paddles. As one can imagine, they were carefully engineered to keep in place and withstand the elements. After two kayaks were secured with long poles and bolted on the inside, the third kayak on each flower petal was lifted into place with a crane.

ROUNDABOUT ART

WHAT: Yakaya

WHERE: Riverbend Park, 799 SW Columbia St.

COST: Free

PRO TIP: To learn more about all of the roundabout art in town, pick up a brochure from Visit Bend. After you see many of them, you can return to the visitor's center and take a short quiz to get a prize!

Bend will have over 50 roundabouts by the time this is published, and roughly half of them have art installations. That's a lot of art to see!

Yakaya *on a beautiful Bend day*

Pillow, who lives in Seattle, has unique sculptures placed in many locations around the country. He randomly came up with the name Yakaya. However, perhaps the name came to him unconsciously because Ya', signifies water in Kaqchikel, a Mayan dialect, and of course, "Kaya" could be short for kayak. It makes perfect sense to place this distinctive piece of art in Riverbend Park, the most popular destination to launch and float the Deschutes River.

THE SHIRE OF BEND

Is there really a *Lord of the Rings*-inspired neighborhood in Bend?

The spirit of J.R.R. Tolkien remains alive and well in a local Bend neighborhood. Inspired by *The Lord of the Rings* trilogy, developer Ron Meyers originally had an idea to create an entire village-like neighborhood of 31 homes. Each home in his ambitious real estate venture would have unique stonework, thatched roofs, terraced gardens, Hobbit holes, and an intricate network of streams and ponds reminiscent of Tolkien's fantasy world.

Unfortunately, a housing crisis hit almost every part of the United States in the early 2000s, and it really hurt Bend's economy. Values of homes plummeted. The vision of the Shire disappeared not long after it had started.

Meyers was able to sell his share of the development to a St. Charles physician. Soon afterward, tragedy also struck the doctor. By the end of the venture only two of the planned homes were built in the Old World style. The rebranded neighborhood became Forest Creek where many nice houses now exist, but they bear no mark of fantasy.

THE LORD OF THE RINGS

WHAT: The Shire of Bend

WHERE: Shire Ln. and Ring Bearer Ct.

COST: Free

PRO TIP: If you decide to drive by these homes, remember they are private residences. People live in them, so please be respectful. Pass through quietly and *do not trespass*.

Did you know you can visit the real Hobbit Houses? Hobbiton, New Zealand, has tours of the movie set available. Get your plane tickets!

34

A private residence inspired by The Lord of the Rings

Luckily, the grand idea remains visible in the unique architecture of the Butterfly Cottage and one other home. Two streets still bear the name of what could have been—Ring Bearer Court and Shire Lane. Frodo or Bilbo Baggins might not be hanging out in the area, but Tolkien would be proud and appreciate the creative endeavor.

GLORY BE TO BICYCLES!

Where can I pray while getting my bike repaired?

Glory be to bicycles! At Web Cyclery in the Old Stone Church, this is most definitely the motto. Without the signs in front, it's easy to mistake the building for a place of worship, and for more than a century, it was indeed. First Presbyterian originally occupied the structure and remained there for many years. Other churches followed, and each time the congregation outgrew the space and needed more.

The Old Stone Church was built in 1912 in the Gothic and Tudor style. Certainly the large tuff stones are impressive, but the most beautiful and ornate designs of the building are its stained glass windows. Deep, multicolored hues with multiple depictions of Jesus and other biblical symbolism light up the inside. The famous Bend logo seal is part of the largest window and rests right on top in the center while emanating

Grace and Hammer in Redmond converted a church into one of the town's best pizza places. Glory be to pizza pies!

Stained glass, Jesus, bicycles, and more!

OLD STONE CHURCH

WHAT: Web Cyclery

WHERE: 157 NW Franklin

COST: Free unless you need a bike or some new skis!

PRO TIP: Stop by to admire the beautiful, intricately designed stained glassed windows. Might as well check out the bikes and skis while you're there!

a respect not only for Christianity but for the city itself.

In the 1980s the roof of the church burned. Of course, it was rebuilt, and over the years many renovations and upgrades have been added. In 2006 the building became a performing arts center for a brief period.

These days, where churchgoers once praised the Lord, bicyclists and outdoor winter enthusiasts applaud the skills of the mechanics and purchase high-caliber bikes and skis. While browsing the shop or waiting on a repair, they can sip a beer from the keg. Nearby, Jesus merrily and miraculously rides a bike with no hands while watching the events of the day.

BEGINNING OF THE BREWS

All these breweries in Central Oregon! Which one was first?

Beer is a way of life in the Pacific Northwest, and Bend is known as one of the most innovative spots in the country for brewing. The water, the hops, the ingenuity of local brewers—all of these factors combine to produce a stellar destination for the tasty beverage.

It all started in 1974 when the McMenamins brothers opened Produce Row Cafe in Portland, the first post-Prohibition brewpub in Oregon. A little more than a decade later, in 1988, Gary Fish opened Deschutes Brewery in Bend. Today, Deschutes is still going and stronger than ever.

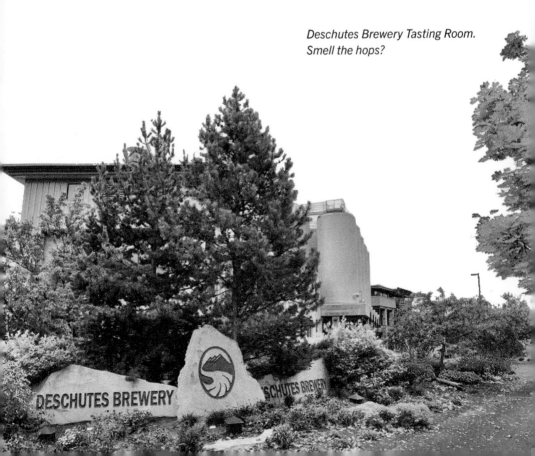

Deschutes Brewery Tasting Room. Smell the hops?

Currently one of the biggest microbreweries in the United States, you can find beers from Deschutes all over the country. You're also likely to see their most popular beers at most festivals and events in Central Oregon.

Located near the Deschutes River, the Bend Tasting Room and Beer Garden has a brewing facility that offers plenty of samples, a relaxed vibe, souvenirs to take home, and often food trucks. On a windy day, the sweet smell of hops from the brewery often permeates the air in the entire nearby area.

The original location in downtown Bend, the Deschutes Brewery & Public House, has many beers and a variety of tasty food. Best to try both locations. Afterward, you'll understand why this institution has become so popular and sparked the beer craze that exists today in Central Oregon.

BEND'S FIRST BREWERY

WHAT: Deschutes Brewery (& Deschutes Public House)

WHERE: 1044 NW Bond St. (901 SW Simpson Ave.)

COST: Depends. Drinking, eating, or both?

PRO TIP: Take an informative and entertaining tour of the brewing facility at the Bend Tasting Room and Beer. Garden You'll walk away a beerologist!

Although Deschutes Brewery was first, Bend has become inundated with amazing breweries. Get yourself a Bend Ale Trail passport and explore them all!

HOMESTEADING DAYS

What is the old wood structure at the Riley Ranch Reserve?

At the Riley Ranch Reserve remnants of a cabin from the Oregon homesteading days sit quietly, slowly deteriorating from time and the elements. Meanwhile, the tranquil flow of the Deschutes can be heard nearby. A short walk leads right to the edge of the river.

How peaceful it must have been living here back in the day. Few people, no traffic (or roundabouts), and an almost untouched, pristine landscape.

Then again, it wasn't the easiest life. In fact, it's difficult for us to imagine the many problems homesteaders faced when they first arrived to the High Desert. Life was hard, and very few settlers remained. Some returned to an easier life back East, while others simply did not survive. One must admire the fortitude of those pioneers—the desire to start a new life, the drive to build something from nothing, and the hope for a better future.

The Riley Reserve is named after O.B. Riley, the fellow who laid claim to the land and built the cabin in the late 1800s. Two hundred years later, it's pretty fascinating that part of the structure still exists, even if it is only a small remnant.

While visiting the cabin, hikers walk the Canyon Loop, a beautiful trail with plentiful views of the Cascades. For a longer stroll, the path connects to Tumalo State Park. Along the way, you can see where Tumalo Creek flows into the Deschutes River.

The Donation Land Claim Act of 1850 (a precursor to other Homesteading Acts) gave up to 320 acres of free land to white males and up to 640 to married couples. It brought approximately 30,000 new settlers to Oregon!

Walking along the trail leads to remnants of O.B. Riley's cabin.

REMNANTS OF A PIONEER

WHAT: Old homesteading cabins

WHERE: Riley Ranch Reserve, 19975 Glen Vista Rd.

COST: Free

PRO TIP: To get an idea of how life used to be, check out one of the best books about the area, *The Oregon Desert* by E.R. Jackman and R.A. Long, Caxton Press, 1964.

The homesteaders deserved these prime locations along the river. Many changes have happened in Central Oregon since those days, but if not for their persistence, Bend would not be what it is today. When I see the cabin at Riley Ranch or other traces of the past, I am grateful for those who paved the way. I often wonder if I could have survived.

BEND OLD IRON WORKS

What is the Old Iron Works District?

At one time almost every aspect of Bend had something to do with the lumber mills, including the area known as the Old Iron Works Arts District. What does iron have to do with lumber, you ask? These industrial buildings once housed foundries that produced cast-iron parts for milling, logging, and mining machinery. In fact, at one point the area was said to be the largest ironwork producer in the entire Pacific Northwest!

Fast forward to the present, and the 2-acre property is still used for production, albeit a type much more fun and creative. Currently, several businesses occupy the historical buildings. This eclectic group offers everything from pastries, jewelry, and home improvement materials to vintage clothing and cacti. With its own delicious signature pastries and drinks, Café des Chutes has quickly and deliciously filled the void left by well-known Sparrow Bakery. The Workhouse hosts a collective of creative locals who produce the most unique items and souvenirs you can find in Bend. Mud Lake Studios offers classes and studio space for creatives. Desert Rose Cactus Lounge has some of the coolest cacti from all parts of the world.

A COLLECTIVE OF CREATIVITY

WHAT: Old Iron Works District

WHERE: 50 SE Scott St.

COST: When shopping, prices vary

PRO TIP: Before purchasing gifts or houseware items at a chain store, visit the shops in the Old Iron District. You will be glad you did!

The Workhouse often offers art classes. A favorite is the Drinker Card, where you learn to paint with only coffee and water!

The Café des Chutes is a great way to start off the day!

The artist-centric Old Iron Works District also occasionally hosts holiday and summer night artist markets, live music, and other regular events. Truthfully, this area of town might possibly be the most creative spot in Bend!

ONE FLEW OVER THE CUCKOO'S NEST

What is the fascination with the author Ken Kesey at Worthy Brewing?

Bend has earned quite a reputation as a beer-lover's mecca. We even have the cool, authentic looking Bend Ale Trail passport that can be stamped at the breweries. Each place has a unique vibe, but one in particular stands out in many exciting ways.

At Worthy Brewing visitors can get a galactic experience at the Hopservatory. A psychedelic-looking mosaic pizza oven churns out some of the best pizza pies in town. The Worthy Garden teaches about conservation and the importance of native species, many of which are growing right out front in raised beds and greenhouses.

Avid readers and movie buffs might be familiar with Ken Kesey, Oregon's most popular author (after me, of course). He wrote the novel *One Flew Over the Cuckoo's Nest*, which was later adapted into a film starring a young and playful Jack Nicholson.

At Worthy, memorabilia featuring Nicholson and Kesey are strewn throughout the building. In fact, the Douglas Fir used for the bar tops, tabletops, and benches may look like ordinary wood, but it was sourced

---

Worthy History Pub often teams up with the Deschutes Historical Museum to offer talks about interesting topics related to Central Oregon's past. Beer and history go great together!

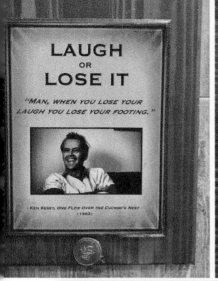

LAUGH
OR
LOSE IT

*"MAN, WHEN YOU LOSE YOUR
LAUGH YOU LOSE YOUR FOOTING."*

- KEN KESEY, ONE FLEW OVER THE CUCKOO'S NEST -
(1962)

EVEN WHEN BEER WAS BAD
IT WAS GOOD

"WE'D JUST SHARED THE LAST BEER AND SLUNG
THE EMPTY CAN OUT THE WINDOW AT A STOP SIGN
AND WERE JUST LEANING BACK TO GET THE FEEL
OF THE DAY, SWIMMING IN THAT KIND OF TASTY
DROWSINESS THAT COMES OVER YOU AFTER A DAY
OF GOING HARD AT SOMETHING YOU ENJOY DOING
-- HALF SUNBURNED AND HALF DRUNK AND
KEEPING AWAKE ONLY BECAUSE
YOU WANTED TO SAVOR THE TASTE
AS LONG AS YOU COULD."

- KEN KESEY, ONE FLEW OVER THE CUCKOO'S NEST -
(1962)

Memorabilia from the 1975 film that won best picture

ONE FLEW OVER THE CUCKOO'S NEST

WHAT: Worthy Brewing

WHERE: 495 NE Bellevue Dr.

COST: Free to view, meals and drinks vary

PRO TIP: Worthy Gardens, a steward of the environment, has its own nursery! Check out Wintercreek Nursery for native plants and gardening ideas in the High Desert.

from the Oregon Mental Hospital where the 1975 Oscar-winning Best Picture was filmed! To discover exactly which pieces of wood, keep a lookout for the certified Cuckoo seal.

Movie souvenirs, Nurse Ratched's signed photo, plaques with quotes, and other mementos also share fun facts about the movie and the author. Even Ken Babbs, Kesey's companion in the Merry Pranksters, has made appearances to give presentations and answer questions about the wild times they shared together. Roger Worthington, owner and founder of the brewery, has definitely proved himself a superfan. His efforts have kept Kesey's spirit alive and well at Worthy.

ALLEY ART

Should I avoid the downtown alleys in Bend?

In many cities people avoid the alleys. Dark, dirty and dangerous, they are usually not known as places to hang out and enjoy the scenery. Not so with the alleys of Bend, especially the one known as Tin Pan Alley. A stroll down this side street leads to colorful art like *The Visitor* by Carol Sternkopf, the small silhouette that might or might not be Bob Dylan (no one can agree), and other creative works. You might even encounter a movie night happening thanks to Tin Pan Theater or stumble upon San Simon, one of Bend's coolest bars.

Though there's only one Tin Pan Alley, other streets downtown have pieces of art and character as well, with recent additions being added from time to time. For example, in Gasoline Alley hang a few paintings like the *Snowpocalypse 2017*, created by Vicki Roadman as a reminder of the rough winter that year. Even the parking garages downtown are spruced up with art!

In fact, the idea became so popular that the Tin Pan Alley movement has spilled over into other parts of the city like the Old Mill District. There you can find works by Megan Marie Myers,

DOWNTOWN ALLEY ART

WHAT: Tin Pan Alley Art

WHERE: Downtown, the Old Mill District

COST: Free

PRO TIP: After loitering in the alleys of downtown, check out other Tin Pan Alley Art pieces in the Old Mill.

On the First Friday of every month, downtown is alive and kicking more than usual! Many galleries and shops stay open later and offer live music, drinks, snacks, and fun.

Art found in the alleys of Bend.
Top: Dawn of a New Day *by*
Megan Phallon Right. *Bob Dylan?*
Lou Reed? Nobody knows for sure
about this anonymous work!

Yuya Negishu, and Danny
Fry. A set of stairs near Ben
& Jerry's are the most artistic
you'll ever climb.

Bend has a deep respect
for artists and allows them to liven up the city with their creativity. Great
for the artists to share their visions, and great for us to view and enjoy!

47

SELFIES WITH CELEBRITIES

Can I really see so many famous musical artists in one place?

Want to hang out or take a selfie with your favorite famous musical artist? Chances are you can meet and greet them at Silver Moon Brewing. Filling one of the huge outside walls at the brewery, the mural *Mix Tape* depicts countless influential artists in many genres of music: James Brown, Britney Spears, Dolly Parton, Metallica, Snoop Dogg, the Beastie Boys, and countless other musicians. Even talented, well-known locals like Mosley Wotta get to hang with the celebrity crowd.

The caricatures look exactly like the real deal. Erik Hoogan, the creative mind behind the mural, follows the age-old adage, "Music is the universal language that brings us all together." When visiting Bend or Silver Moon, especially for the first time, it's always entertaining to play the "Guess as many artists as possible" game. Consider it a true test to prove who reigns as king or queen of pop culture. Repeat visitors

CELEBRITY PARTY

WHAT: The *Mix Tape* mural at Silver Moon Brewing

WHERE: 24 NW Greenwood Ave.

COST: You know you'll want to try a beer or a food cart, so it all depends on what you want to spend.

PRO TIP: Silver Moon hosts a variety of concerts and comedy, and their trivia night is off the chain. The brewery has definitely become one of the best spots to hang out in Bend.

Want to know a secret? Locals night is Monday at Silver Moon, and they have the best drink specials in town!

A small section of the lifelike and amazing mural Mix Tape *by Erik Hoogan*

often admire and discuss the mural as well, and live concerts happen regularly at the brewery. Did I mention Silver Moon also has a great food truck lot called The Office?

Anyone can easily see that Hoogan's musical vision has certainly helped bring folks together. While there, you might as well try some of the best beers in Bend, another universal language that breaks down borders and unites humankind.

FUJIOKA, THE JAPANESE SISTER CITY OF BEND

Why are there two giant stones in the middle of the walkway downtown?

Careful—don't trip on those two giant rocks downtown! Yes, they're right in the middle of the walkway in front of Bellatazza, but those rocks were placed there for a reason. They represent the bond between the far away city of Fujioka, Japan, and Bend, Oregon.

Fujioka is Bend's sister city. With a population of around 65,000, it has about as many people as Bend did last week (just kidding, but we all know Bend is growing at a ridiculously quick pace). Like Bend, the city seems to be a nature-lover's paradise. They get a lot more rain than we do, and in the spring, they celebrate the magnificent blooms of wisteria. If you're lucky enough to be familiar with this smell, it's one of the sweetest, most fragrant aromas of any flower in the world. In fact, the name Fujioka translates to "wisteria hill."

Over the years, students from Bend and Fujioka have participated in exchange programs and visited each other's cities. Bend students toured Toyota, tried Japanese papermaking, and soaked up other parts of this fascinating culture. Fujioka students visited the High Desert Museum, the Lava Lands, and even Pine Tavern!

The two cities exchanged one half of a native stone to create a similar sculpture, so somewhere in Fujioka people are also tripping on rocks and wondering why they are there. The rock dedication in Bend took place in 2005.

Apparently, Fujioka is also similar to Bend because it has lots of nearby hiking, biking, kayaking and other outdoor activities.

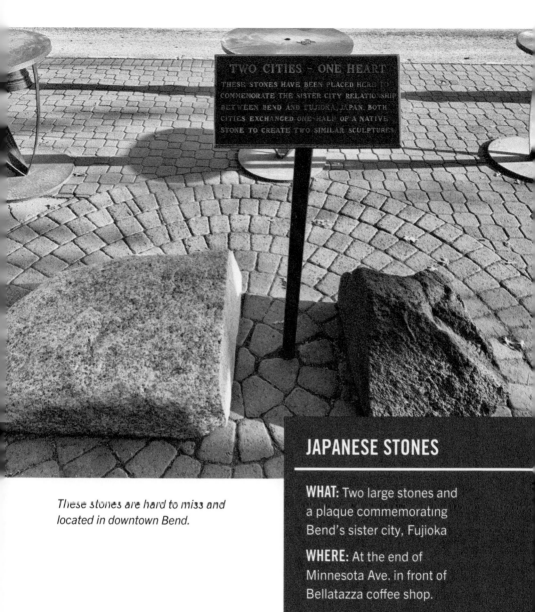

TWO CITIES - ONE HEART

THESE STONES HAVE BEEN PLACED HERE TO
COMMEMORATE THE SISTER CITY RELATIONSHIP
BETWEEN BEND AND FUJIOKA, JAPAN. BOTH
CITIES EXCHANGED ONE-HALF OF A NATIVE
STONE TO CREATE TWO SIMILAR SCULPTURES

These stones are hard to miss and located in downtown Bend.

JAPANESE STONES

WHAT: Two large stones and a plaque commemorating Bend's sister city, Fujioka

WHERE: At the end of Minnesota Ave. in front of Bellatazza coffee shop.

COST: Free

PRO TIP: Check out some pictures of Fujioka, Japan. It's a beautiful place, especially when the wisteria is in bloom.

I'm not sure if students still travel between our two cities but Fujioka certainly has enough natural beauty to make anyone want to add it to their bucket list.

THE HIGH DESERT MUSEUM

Where is the best spot to take kids in Central Oregon?

Otters, raptors, and porcupines, oh my! Ask most every kid who has been there, and they'll put the High Desert Museum (HDM) as their top spot to visit in Central Oregon.

Usually those cute, furry critters like the gray fox, the eerie-looking barn owl, and other native animals are well hidden in the High Desert, but not at this museum. Ever seen a Bald Eagle or a porcupine close up? A chuckwalla? Yeah, me neither. I didn't know what a chuckwalla was until I saw one in the Desertarium. Even better, these animals are often rescued and well taken care of at the HDM for the remainder of their days.

More than animals, permanent exhibits follow the integral peoples of High Desert history. The Spirit of the West begins with a lifelike journey through the times of the indigenous Paiute culture who first lived on this land and navigates through

You can adopt an animal at the High Desert Museum! No, they won't let you take it home, but donations help pay for your animal's food and care. With some donations, you even get a one-on-one meeting with your adoptee.

Isn't this little gray fox cute?

the days of fur trappers, Chinese immigrants, and on up to the present. The High Desert Ranch and Sawmill exhibits the rough and tough lifestyle of homesteaders and others who settled here years ago, with replicas of an old-school outhouse, a willow corral, a cabin, and more.

Trails on the property lead through the ponderosa pine, rabbitbrush, and other native species with signage that explains the importance of natural habitats, forest fires, the riparian system of rivers and lakes, and other important aspects of the local environment. Changing exhibits allow you to return to the museum and always discover something new. There is no other place in Central Oregon where you can learn as much about the High Desert region in such an interactive, exciting way.

STYLISH STATUES

Who dresses up the Centennial Logger?

Of all the roundabout art in Bend, one guy seems to get more preferential treatment than others. Could it be his good looks? His calm demeanor? Whatever the reason, we often see him dressed for the seasons and especially on holidays.

His name is Bob. No, not really, but we should give him a legit name. He's simply called the Centennial Logger, and he's a bronze statue that was created for Bend's centennial celebration.

During Christmas he is likely to be wearing a Santa hat. He dresses in green on St. Patty's Day, and might sport some shorts and a Hawaiian shirt in summer. I'm pretty sure I've seen him wearing Mardi Gras beads a couple of times.

At first, I thought maybe the Arts in Public Places organization (AiPP) was responsible for Bob's, I mean the Logger's, flashy attire. Surely the Bend police weren't looking the other way as drunken locals surreptitiously changed his clothes during the wee hours of the night, or rambunctious teenagers were

STATUE DRESS UP

WHAT: The Centennial Logger

WHERE: Roundabout at Reed Market

COST: Free

PRO TIP: If you want to get a close up-look at this fella, park at Farewell Bend Park. It's not a good idea to stop in the middle of a roundabout!

I often wonder if his buddy down the road, the Centennial Planter, gets jealous. This guy gets dressed up at times, but not as often, poor fella. Any one feel like sneaking out one night to play wardrobe specialist?

pulling a prank. I mean, it's harmless fun and sounds like something I would have done as a kid. It is, in fact, different groups of community members who get together from time to time and decide to dress him up to spread cheer to the rest of us. I, for one, always look forward to his latest fashion.

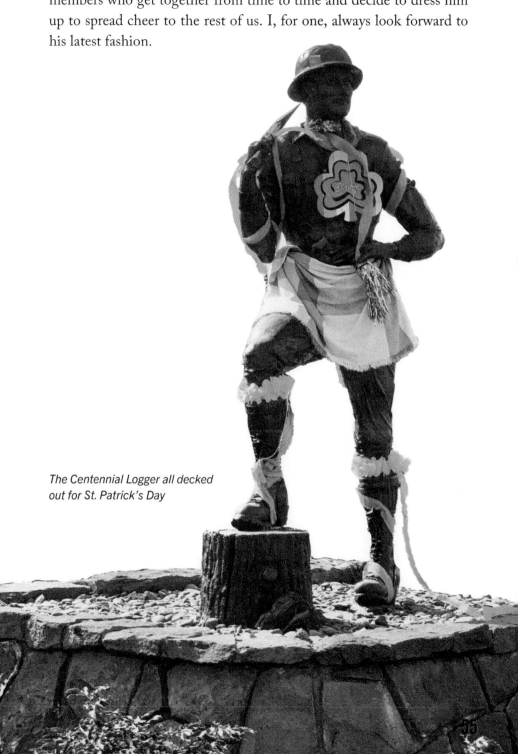

The Centennial Logger all decked out for St. Patrick's Day

RELIVING THE OREGON TRAIL

Looking to relive the Oregon Trail?

Before Call of Duty and even before Super Mario Brothers, I was dying of dysentery on The Oregon Trail. Remember the classic computer game? Players could choose to be a farmer, a banker, or a carpenter. Then you would get some startup money to buy oxen, food, and other supplies. To the tune of Yankee Doodle, the journey would begin! I can still hear the sound of the wagon wheels in my head.

Along the way, players would actually learn quite a bit about the trials and tribulations of those who made the grueling trip from Independence, Missouri, to the Pacific Northwest. Those were the days!

I never thought I'd end up living in Oregon, much less get to see parts of the authentic Oregon Trail. Although the original route runs a good ways north of Bend, the Huntington Wagon Road is the closest we have to trailblazing history here.

In 1864 the government signed a treaty with the Paiute, Modoc, and Klamath tribes. A few years later, the Klamath Indian Reservation was created. Part of the agreement required

The dusty Huntington Wagon Road

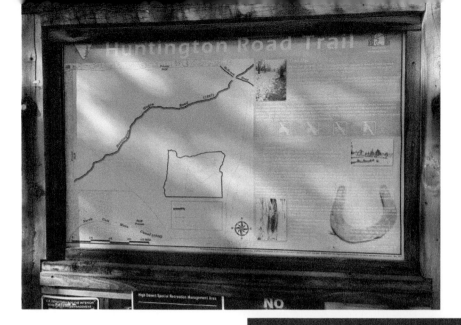

A place marker with info about the history of the trail

PIONEER ROADS

WHAT: Huntington Wagon Road

WHERE: Off the beaten path on McGrath Road. Best to type in "Huntington Wagon Trail" in the GPS. You'll get there.

COST: Free

PRO TIP: The Oregon Trail game is still fun to play online! Go to: visitoregon.com/the-oregon-trail-game-online

the government to provide the Indians with supplies, which came from the Dalles. From the Dalles to Fort Klamath soldiers, immigrants and others utilized the route that became the Huntington Wagon Road. Here in Central Oregon, they traversed through junipers, sagebrush, and other local vegetation.

As runners and hikers explore the area, they can pretend to be travelers on the Oregon Trail ready to settle large homesteads. The area is quiet and rarely crowded, so even if hikers talk to themselves about low rations or what they need to be successful in the harsh new land, no one is around to hear.

Artifacts from the past have been found on the trail, and many of them are located at the Deschutes Historical Museum.

LAVA BEARS

Is there really such a thing as a Lava Bear?

Here in the Pacific Northwest, the belief in the mythical Bigfoot still lingers. Who knows what other superstitions the Pacific Northwesterners believe, but at one time, they thought the Lava Bear was supposedly a real, distinct type of creature seen only in Oregon. Often living among the lava beds, these poor animals were small because the harsh environment stunted their growth. With little food or water, one can imagine their difficult plight.

A fella named Alfred Andrews trapped the first supposed Lava Bear in 1923, and a few others were subsequently trapped over the next 10 years or so. After further study, scientists have since decided that they were never really a separate species, but rather a variety of the American black bear. They agreed the critters were likely so small because of malnutrition.

The Lava Bear has lived on in spirit since 1930 as the Bend High School mascot. In fact, the bears might be more popular and ferocious now than they were back then. A statue at the roundabout near Bend High is technically a Grizzly, and way more ferocious than any of the real bears would

FEROCIOUS MASCOT

WHAT: A statue of the Lava Bear

WHERE: Located at the Franklin Avenue and 15th Street Roundabout

COST: Free

PRO TIP: Don't ever tell a Bend High student or alumni this story. Let them keep thinking the Lava Bear is the most ferocious mascot in Oregon.

Lava Bears, Bigfoot, alien festivals in McMinnville; Oregon is full of legends and the "unknown."

have been. Still, most locals assume it's just what a Lava Bear looked like.

If any of these beasts exist nowadays, they are probably hanging out with Bigfoot in the deepest parts of the forest or caves. Get a pic of both of them together and you might make a small fortune.

The bronze Lava Bear located at the Franklin and 15th Street Roundabout

A DOWNTOWN FOREST

Have you ever noticed the forest in downtown Bend?

Many people pass the corner of Wall Street and Franklin Avenue in downtown Bend without ever noticing that they just walked through a forest. Say what? Yes, we know there are many forests nearby. And sure, there are nicely manicured trees scattered about downtown, but this forest has no pine needles or leaves to clean up, nor does it offer any shade on a hot, sunny day.

If meanderers even bother to look around, they likely see a sign for the Franklin Crossing Building and a real estate office with flyers for some of the latest, most luxurious, and most expensive residential listings in Central Oregon.

A closer look at eye level reveals Bend's downtown forest. Bronze plaques with golden, imprinted specimens of native species like the western juniper, the ponderosa pine, and others are placed all around the building.

And surely you know the Latin names? If not, time to memorize them and impress your friends next

HIDDEN IN PLAIN SIGHT

WHAT: Plaques with the name of many native tree species

WHERE: The Franklin Building

COST: Free

PRO TIP: As cool as the plaques are, the real fun is seeing these specimens in the real forest. Get outside!

Speaking of so many trees in one area, here's a fun fact: Over 40,000 aspens located in Utah make up the largest group of trees in the entire world. Pando, as this group was named, is believed to be the largest, most dense living organism ever found!

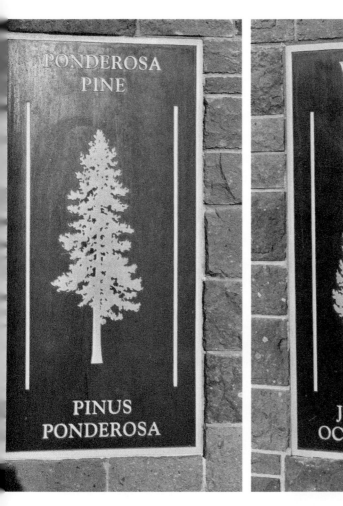

Two of the many small plaques located on the Franklin Building in downtown Bend.

time a random conversation about local trees comes up. That's a *Juniperus occidentalis*, silly! You didn't know?

The downtown forest is a good way to see so many native trees in such close proximity, and to get a good idea of what they really look like. Just don't expect to throw down a blanket in the shade for a picnic!

A RAINBOW OF BOTTLES

Who stuck those random glass bottles in the side of that building?!

Of all the places to put old, antique bottles, why not fill an empty hole with them? This is exactly what Jacqueline Smith, the owner of Found Natural Goods, decided to do at her downtown gift shop.

The downtown building on Brooks had a large hole in the wall courtesy of one of those old school A/C units. Of course, after it was removed, she had to fill it, but how?

It just so happened that her family had a small ranch in Alfalfa, Oregon. One day, a hailstorm came along and annihilated an old barn on the property. Sounds terrible, but underneath the barn was a treasure trove full of literally hundreds of antique bottles—green, amber, blue, clear, big, and small. Most likely the area had been a spot where people buried their trash.

All those colorful bottles needed a home, and the large hole at her shop needed to be filled. Jacqueline killed two birds with one stone by creating an eco-friendly solution inspired by the colorful art she had come to appreciate in places like Mexico and the southwest United States.

A COLORFUL ADDITION

WHAT: A bunch of colorful glass bottles stuck in the side of a building

WHERE: Found Natural Goods, 1001 NW Brooks St.

COST: Free to view, money to shop

PRO TIP: Found Natural Goods is located between two hot spots in Bend, Pine Tavern and Bend Brewing. If you haven't been to one (or both) of those, you're missing out!

You may want to keep old bottles, especially those unique ones. People collect almost everything, and one of them might fetch more than a 10-cent recycling fee.

These colorful bottles are found on the side of Found Natural Goods located in downtown Bend.

The shop, Found Natural Goods, began as a website in 2014 with just six products from the Badlands: tumbleweeds, arrowheads, deer sheds, juniper berries, and sage smudge sticks. The brick and mortar store opened in 2018 with just eight local artists and has since expanded rapidly to more than 120 businesses from all over the states, including many local and female artists. Inside, you might not be able to purchase the colorful, old bottles in the wall, but an abundance of other unique treasures await.

BEAR HUGS AND BEER

Where can you get a big bear hug and a beer in the same spot?

It's certainly a question I ask myself often. Don't you? Hugs and beer, two of the most comforting things in life.

At Newport Avenue Market, quite a few quirky objects await. I mentioned the bear, a bronze, lovable looking fella that sits awaiting hugs on the outside of the building. Nearby but not quite as noticeable is the tombstone that states, "The Year a Sense of Humor Died," a tribute to a time when not everyone was so sensitive (I hope I don't get canceled for saying that).

Meanwhile, the Bend Wall mural pops with color in the background. The city's most iconic mural (and popular selfie post) was painted by local artist Kim Smallenberg. At 100 feet wide by 20 feet tall, it features Central Oregon hotspots like Mount Bachelor, Tumalo Falls, and Tower Theatre. Look closely enough and you might notice that the painting even pays homage to the Great American Eclipse of 2017.

The fun doesn't stop there. Inside, another softer and furrier bear named Francine Bearbottom greets customers. Keep an eye out for the shiny,

The Newport Market sign out front in the parking lot always has some silly but funny saying or joke. Be sure to check it out while you're there.

The Bend Wall mural at Newport Avenue Market by Kim Smallenburg

life-sized purple cow named Viris (Violet + Iris = Viris). She's the Newport Market's mascot. And did I mention the "Beer Wall," the largest selection of beers in Bend?

With all these eccentricities you're guaranteed to get more out of a trip to the market than just groceries.

NEWPORT AVENUE MARKET

WHAT: The Bend Mural, beer, bears, and more

WHERE: Newport Avenue Market, 1121 NW Newport Ave.

COST: Might as well stock up on groceries while there.

PRO TIP: This is Bend's best local market. I mentioned the beer wall, and I could go on about the cheesery, the bakery, the . . .

THE LAST BLOCKBUSTER

**If my streaming service doesn't have the movies
I want to watch, where can I still find them?**

Blockbuster Video has become a worldwide phenomenon. No, not the once mighty franchise, but the lone, single store, the only one left in the ENTIRE world. If you've never heard anything else about Bend, Oregon, you probably know we have the last Blockbuster.

A documentary and then a TV show on Netflix (ironic, right?) helped to rekindle the fascination with this cultural icon. The 2022 Super Bowl commercial, though only shown online, added more fuel to the growing popularity. It featured the end of the world, and only two things still existed: cockroaches and Blockbuster!

BLAST FROM THE PAST

WHAT: The Last Blockbuster Video

WHERE: 211 NE Revere Ave., #3

COST: Rentals, souvenirs vary

PRO TIP: Don't just visit; get a membership card and rent a movie!

For those of us who grew up with cassettes, VHS, and DVDs, Blockbuster is truly a place to relive those days when we spent weekend nights scouring the aisles for movies to watch. The store also has souvenirs galore, including books by yours truly, sweatpants, shot glasses, magnets, and anything else you might cherish as a keepsake. Memorabilia from

Blockbuster popped up in a recent episode of *Family Guy* as well. The Griffins take a road trip all the way to Bend to rent a VHS! But beware, the store only has DVDs and Blu-rays.

Everyone likes to take a pic in front of the World's Last Blockbuster sign!

Russell Crowe's film *Robin Hood*, Denzel Washington's actor's chair from *American Gangster*, autographs, and other movie mementos fill glass cases. Hopefully, items like this will continue to accumulate and eventually we might end up with a really cool film museum of sorts.

And of course, movies! Blockbuster still carries new DVD and Blu-ray releases and many of our older favorites. Personally, I still enjoy walking the aisles to find something cool to rent. It's easy to discover a film that can't be found on one of the growing list of streaming services. Plus, rental prices are cheaper, and there is no substitute for nostalgia.

BIRD WATCHING AT ITS BEST

Where is the best spot in Central Oregon to go bird watching?

Attention bird enthusiasts! Grab your binoculars, a spotting scope, and a field guide, and head to Hatfield Ponds to see birds galore. In fact, according to eBird, a popular website for bird watchers, over 250 species have been seen at Hatfield!

HATFIELD PONDS

WHAT: Bird watching

WHERE: 22395 McGrath Rd.

COST: Free

PRO TIP: Download the eBird or Merlin app to get the best idea of what you are viewing or to keep a digital checklist. Warning, this can become an addictive pastime!

This area on the east side of town is mostly undeveloped and is known for Bend's small municipal airport. Perhaps some people are aware it is the site of Bend's wastewater facility, which treats dirty water that is then used for irrigation and such. Percolation ponds are formed as part of the treatment process and thus, the Hatfield Ponds.

These small bodies of water are magnets for our beautiful, feathered friends. Waterfowl like Canadian geese and a variety of ducks are seen frequently, but so are numerous others not seen anywhere else in Central Oregon. Cattails and other vegetation that border the ponds provide cover and a nesting habitat for sora, Virginia rail, and the marsh wren. There are also osprey, blue heron, kinglets, bluebirds . . .

Don't be surprised if someone approaches and asks if you've seen the rare Green Heron. There are some serious enthusiasts out there!

Bird watching and majestic mountain views at Hatfield Ponds

A small wooden box near the trailhead has a birding checklist of species seen in the area. Longtime birders claim that spring and fall are the best times of year to spot the widest variety, but almost any time of year offers prime viewing. As an added bonus, both the short hike around the water and the view of the Cascades in the backdrop are pretty amazing.

A LAYOVER AT THE CAVES

What should I do while waiting for my flight at the Redmond airport?

No one really likes those boring layovers at the airports. It can be fun to pass the time people watching, grabbing a coffee or beer, or catching up on podcasts, but only for so long. Why not hang out at some cool caves instead?

Seriously, the Redmond Caves are very close to the airport, walking distance in fact, and definitely better than sitting around the terminal for hours. These ancient lava tubes are found all around Deschutes County, with the ones in Redmond located the farthest north. Part of the larger Horse Lava Tube system of caves (122 at last count), they were formed by the volcanic flow of molten lava from the Newbery Caldera 80,000 years ago, give or take a few years.

A short trail surrounded by sagebrush, bitterbrush, juniper trees, and other native vegetation leads to the caves by the airport.

THE ROCK COLLECTOR

WHAT: Redmond Caves

WHERE: SE Airport Way, Redmond

COST: Free

PRO TIP: Take a flashlight, a jacket, and plenty of water, especially when planning to explore the caves for any significant length of time.

Deep inside the Siskiyou Mountains are the Marble Halls of Oregon. These are part of the Oregon Caves National Monument and worth a visit!

One of the several Redmond Caves near the airport.

Unfortunately, some not-so-smart humans have graffitied some parts, but no worries—bad karma will overtake them one day. Still, the caves are pretty fascinating, and they make the curious wonder what else might be underground to explore.

The Redmond Caves are open year-round. During hot summer days the temperature inside of them is colder, so they offer a welcome reprieve from the blistering sun. Just make sure to get back in time for your flight!

THE DRY CANYON

Why does part of the Dry Canyon in Redmond look like a garbage dump?

Through the middle of Redmond runs what was once an ancient river. It's called the Dry Canyon now because, well, it's a dry canyon. Nevertheless, the area still gets used by locals for playing disc golf, biking, running, and meandering on pleasant days. Nearby are a skatepark and a playground. In the middle of the canyon, the arch of the Maple Street Bridge has handholds and footholds where people can get some great climbing practice.

Walking along the entire trail, it's hard not to notice what looks to be a cemetery for rusted car parts, paint cans, and other rubbish from a time not so long ago. When Redmond was a tiny town back in the 1920s this spot was located outside of the city limits. Locals used it as a dump site because it was the closest place to take trash. Remember, citizens back then didn't have a service where huge garbage trucks picked up overflowing plastic trash cans every week. How lucky are we?

The city intended to clean up the canyon and remove the trash, but soon found out that it has basically become part of the landscape! Removing it would destroy the structural integrity of the cliffside and quite possibly send rocks, dirt and other debris tumbling down. I'd hate to be there when that happened!

Walking the almost 4-mile trail through the heart of the Dry Canyon and witnessing the surrounding walls of rimrock is fascinating. Those rocks tell a longer history than the trash!

AN ANCIENT CANYON

WHAT: The Dry Canyon

WHERE: There are a few trailheads for access; Redmond

COST: Free

PRO TIP: Test your strength and endurance climbing the Maple Street Bridge. What a workout!

Top left and right: *Views of the canyon.* Bottom: *The author attempting a climb up the Maple Street Bridge*

So now visitors get a taste of history in the form of trash. Luckily, it's not the kind that smells gross. Honestly, I think it's kind of cool and adds to Redmond's history and character.

THE SURVIVING HOMESTEAD

What is the oldest structure in Deschutes County?

On the Deschutes River, seemingly in the middle of nowhere, an old home sits derelict. But this isn't just any old, dilapidated wood building. The Andrew Jackson Tetherow home is the oldest standing home in all of Deschutes County and one of the oldest in all of Oregon!

The home was built in 1878–79. Andrew Jackson Tetherow (a very popular name at the time and not to be confused with the seventh president) lived there on a ranch with his wife and four children for many years. During this period, the property was used not only as a residence, but also as a waystation for travelers. Over the years it served as an inn, campsite, store, farm, ranch, orchard, garden, dairy, blacksmith, brewery, and probably a few other side hustles. The site was also one of only three river crossings in the early days of settlement, at first by a cable ferry and eventually a bridge. And what's more, the first diversion of water from the Deschutes River for irrigation was on the Tetherow Ranch. This place is full of fascinating history!

THE OLDEST STRUCTURE

WHAT: Andrew Jackson Tetherow Homestead (Tetherow Crossing)

WHERE: SW Helmholtz Way, Redmond

COST: Free

PRO TIP: Pack a lunch and visit on a nice day. The house currently isn't much to look at, but you can chill and have a picnic by the river.

Over all those years many additions and upgrades were added, and the structure was in use until 1999. As of this writing, the home is boarded up and in much need of repair, but the city of Redmond has grand plans for restoration. It's just a matter of raising the funds from donations and such (hint, hint). In truth, the building

Andrew's home is still standing!

would be ideal as a small museum with a park. It's fairly secluded with a large open area of green grass, the perfect little spot to relax with the Deschutes River peacefully flowing in the background.

At one time Redmond had its own museum, and hopefully they will have another in the future. In the meantime, the Deschutes Historical Museum preserves the area's past.

SMITH ROCK, HOLLYWOOD SUPERSTAR

Why does Smith Rock look so familiar?

Smith Rock State Park may look familiar even to those who have never visited. Why? Not only is it a mesmerizingly postcard-perfect landscape, but the area is also Hollywood famous. In fact, it has been used as a location for several well-known movies.

One of the most well-known films is *Wild*, based on the book of the same name and starring Reese Witherspoon. She plays Cheryl Strayed, the author who traverses the PCT (Pacific Coast Trail) in an attempt to put her crazy life back in order. Though most Oregonians know Smith Rock is not technically on the PCT, who can blame the filmmakers for wanting to use such a majestic backdrop? And when has Hollywood ever been known to be 100 percent accurate?

Other films like *Homeward Bound*, *The Postman*, *Swordfish*, *Rooster Cogburn* (with John Wayne), and a few others had scenes shot at the state park as well. For those of us who are familiar with the area, it's

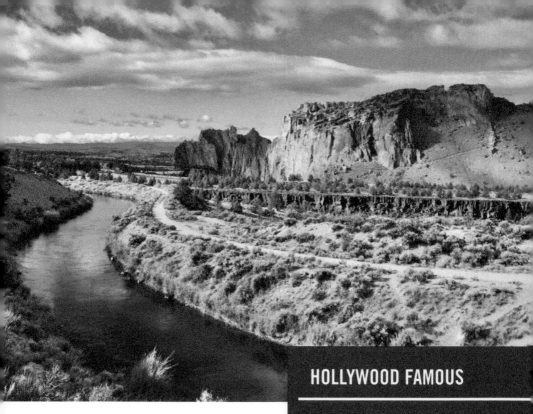

A beautiful day at Smith Rock State Park

fun to see which parts of Central Oregon we recognize in these films. However, movies, like photographs, can never do a landscape justice. Even with really cool Instagram filters, nothing quite compares to witnessing a place firsthand. There is a reason why Smith Rock is one of the most visited state parks in Oregon. If you have not visited, I suggest you put down this book and take a trip immediately.

Test your endurance on Misery Ridge Trail or another spectacular hike and see why Smith Rock is a Hollywood superstar.

A ROCK GARDEN

What exactly is a rock garden, and where can I find one?

On my first visit, I was greeted upon arrival by a barking dog and several peacocks roaming the property. I thought for sure I had gone to the wrong place. A home, perhaps reminiscent of one you might see in a horror film, sat eerily quiet near the entrance.

This only added to the unique vibe of Peterson's Rock Garden, a place where the imagination of a hardworking, homesteading Dane came alive. The garden was created by Rasmus Christian Peterson, an immigrant from Denmark who came West in the 1930s to take advantage of the Desert Land Act. Obviously an eccentric individual, he meticulously created replicas of the Statue of Liberty, the Capitol Building, a schoolhouse, elaborate stone bridges over ponds filled with lily pads, and many more structures from locally sourced stones like obsidian, agate, thundereggs, and others. A true rockhounder!

As Peterson aged, he sold most of his large homestead and devoted his time to his creative hobby. After his death, his wife and family kept the attraction open, and like Peterson, they never charged an admission fee, asking for donations instead.

THE ROCK COLLECTOR

WHAT: Peterson's Rock Garden

WHERE: 7930 SW 77th St., Redmond

COST: Donations requested

PRO TIP: This is the type of place you want to revisit. Every time you go, you will discover something new.

To help with the massive endeavor of restoration, the new owners have days where volunteers can help with cleanup and other maintenance on the grounds. Let's chip in!

For a while, visitors walking the property clearly noticed an unkempt rock garden in need of some serious TLC. Yet even then Peterson's imagination inspired awe. He left behind one of the most unique legacies in Central Oregon. At the time of this writing, new owners are slowly restoring it to its former glory, and they have grand ambitions. Hopefully, future generations will discover a revival close to the original dream of Peterson. Fingers crossed.

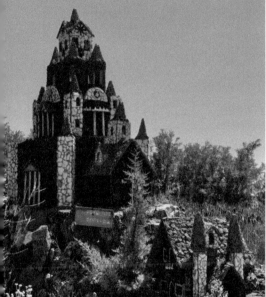

A few of Peterson's amazing rock structures built from his large collection

OLD-SCHOOL MOVIE THEATERS

Where can I get an old-school, unique cinema experience?

Honestly, I think these newer movie theaters with their big sound systems and mega screens are overkill, not to mention super expensive. Try taking a family of four for a night out! I'll take the smaller cinemas with more character any day, and luckily, Central Oregon has a few.

Tin Pan Theater has long been the best place in Bend to see smaller, independent films. Instead of those big-budget, CGI movies, this boutique theater gives us the chance to see the overlooked but usually much better films. In October, the theater hosts the celebrated Bend Film Festival. In summer, you might catch a movie in the outside alley.

McMenamins is well known for several entertaining things, and in Bend, the St. Francis Theater is one of them. Comfortable sofas and a mix of first-run and older films provides a relaxed viewing experience.

Odem Theater Pub in Redmond has been a theater since the 1930s. Located downtown, this spot's large neon sign stands out, especially at night. The selection of food and drink is second to none, and the small movie rooms are intimate and cozy.

The Bend Film Festival held in October is one of the largest, most acclaimed festivals in the entire Pacific Northwest. Many of the films screened at the festival can be seen year-round at Tin Pan Theater.

The entrance to Tin Pan Alley Theater

Finally, let's not forget the old barn, better known as Sisters Movie House. First-run films, good food, and you can even purchase an annual subscription that allows you to view an unlimited number of films, thus guaranteeing you'll always have a conversation starter about popular culture. Next time you visit a cinema, opt for one of these more unique spots.

A COWBOY DINNER

Where can I get the biggest and tastiest piece of meat I've ever eaten?

Vegetarians, go ahead and skip this one. Or not, but beware, I'm about to talk about the largest, most savory, and delicious slabs of meat in all of Central Oregon!

The Cowboy Dinner Tree is literally in the middle of nowhere. The drive takes visitors through the Oregon Outback and endless miles of sagebrush. Once you arrive in the tiny town of Silver Lake (population 123), about a 90-minute drive from Bend, a small shack with the most pleasant aroma awaits. A set meal begins with salad and soup, followed by a huge piece of steak or chicken and a baked potato. You get a big ol' glass of lemonade to wash it all down, and if that's not enough, here comes dessert!

While waiting for a table (or to work off the massive amount of food you just consumed), practice your lasso skills in the courtyard. Meander and watch the sunset or take in the stars after dark. There are no city lights to impede the flawless view of the cosmos.

Onsite camping is available if you don't want to return home in a food coma. Visitors are almost guaranteed to leave with a baggie of leftovers to last for at least the next few days.

DELICIOUS DINNERS

WHAT: Cowboy Dinner Tree

WHERE: Silver Lake

COST: A set price of $80, cash only

PRO TIP: Order the steak. Then, go again and order the chicken.

The nearby area known as Christmas Valley has other unique places to explore, like Fort Rock and Crack in the Ground. Best to make it a road trip!

Top: *The humble but inviting Cowboy Dinner Tree.* Inset: *The author practicing his lasso skills!*

Is your mouth watering yet? It's a good drive to get there, and you had best make reservations way in advance, so stop reading this and get going, partner!

THE OLD MAN

All these huge pine trees! Where is the largest one in Central Oregon?

Many people say Central Oregon has only two types of trees, pines and junipers. And while we see others, these two types of evergreens certainly dominate the High Desert landscape. The juniper is known for its gnarled, rough looking branches. Personally, I don't find the dark blue berries too tasty, but they are a favorite for birds and some mammals. Did you know they are also used to make gin?

Then there are the pines, a genus which includes almost 200 types. Central Oregon has several varieties, including sugar pines, lodgepoles, and the largest—the mighty and majestic ponderosa pines.

Here in Oregon we have the granddaddy of them all. At around 500 years old, 162 feet tall, and with an 8.6-foot diameter, Big Red is the largest and oldest ponderosa pine on record! Due to the passage of time, weather, and unfortunately those evil folks who climb and vandalize

THE OLDEST PINE

WHAT: Big Red, the mightiest of all ponderosa pines!

WHERE: La Pine State Park, 15800 State Recreation Rd., La Pine

COST: Free to see the tree, but day-use or annual State Park pass is required.

PRO TIP: Rarely crowded, La Pine State Park is a great place to go camping. Grab the tent, the kids, and the BBQ!

The town of La Pine often gets overlooked, but is no doubt worth exploring, especially the trails in the state park. Visit the Wetlands Taphouse for some good grub and drink!

Respect this old fella!

it, the tree shows its age. A fence has been built around it for protection, but you can still snap a pic and show this mighty conifer your respect.

The tree is located in La Pine State Park. When you visit, Big Red is not the only thing to experience. The area has plenty of trails for biking, hiking, running, or horse riding. The Deschutes River meanders peacefully through the park, with day-use areas for swimming, floating, or kayaking.

STIMPSON HOUSE

What in the world is that odd structure at the Stimpson House?

Walking leisurely one afternoon around Redmond, I stumbled upon a strange looking structure in the middle of someone's front yard. In a regular looking neighborhood, at an average looking home, this thing stuck out, and I had to get a closer look.

The placard near this apparent work of art states that it is called *Weather Central* and tells quite a comical history if it's to be believed. Made from what appears to be baking pans, fans, bike tires, horns, and other random items, the oddity was probably meant for some purpose, but what it was I have no idea.

Further info mentions the man who created it, H.R. Stimpson. A peculiar acrophobic (fear of heights) fella, he and his wife Natasha purchased this particular house because it had no basement. It seems he was scared of depths and not heights?

H.R. was apparently something of a small-town celebrity in Redmond at one time. He owned a juke joint downtown. Also a singer and songwriter, his song "The Snow Toes Blues" became a local hit and led to the formation of

RECYCLED INTO ART

WHAT: *Weather Central*

WHERE: 1312 SW Evergreen Ave., Redmond

COST: Free

PRO TIP: Like a few other entries in this book, this is someone's residence, so please be respectful when viewing and don't trespass.

Redmond's Art in Public Places is growing steadily. Murals, sculptures, and such can be seen popping up all around town. Never know when you might see something new!

The former home of H.R. Stimpson and his creative Weather Central *sculpture*

Slide Simpson & The New Slide Stimpson Glide Band. The home hosted rehearsals for other aspiring amateur musicians over the years as well, and at one point was dubbed The Central Oregon Home for the Chronically Groovy. Gotta love the name.

WESTERN STYLE TOWN

Why does the entire town of Sisters look like something out of the Old West?

The town of Sisters, Oregon, often called the Gateway to the Cascades, has an allure reminiscent of the American Old West—strange in a town that has only been around since 1901 and was not formally incorporated until 1946. By then, the Old West style had come and gone.

Actually, this "Western" update was a well-planned experiment. For most of its history, Sisters thrived as a lumber town. But by the early 1960s the mills had closed, and the population began to decline. Does this history sound familiar yet?

The 1970s brought new ideas to rebrand and reinvigorate the community. The city council passed an ordinance declaring that businesses should create Western-style storefronts. Brooks Resources, developer of the nearby Black Butte Ranch, offered these businesses a grant of $5,000 to help create the facades. Sure enough, the revival of the Old West began.

Sisters Saloon has been around since 1912!

Today, many locals would argue that the idea worked too well. Sisters has become a tourist magnet. Driving down the main strip on a weekend or during the summer can be slow and frustrating. Watch out for the pedestrians who can't find the proper crosswalks (or just don't care). Nevertheless, the idea stimulated the town's tourist economy, and it certainly has a unique and inviting atmosphere.

Who knows if Sisters would have been so attractive without the Western allure? I would gamble on the yes side, though perhaps not quite as much. After all, the town has charm and character and some unique shops, and it is located near some amazing national wilderness and outdoor recreation.

Where did the name Sisters come from? The town is named after the prominent Cascade peaks of the Three Sisters, which can be seen from town. They are also known as Faith, Hope & Charity.

WORLD WAR II CAMP

Did Sunriver used to be a World War II camp for soldiers?

Folks mostly know Sunriver as a famed resort with tons of activities to keep tourists occupied—vacation homes, golf courses, Sunriver Nature Center, Sunriver Homeowners Aquatic and Recreation Center (SHARC), quick access to the outdoors, and the list keeps rolling . . .

Long before the area became a tourist playground, the grounds where Sunriver Resort now stands were utilized as a camp for soldiers during World War II. Because the forest, river, and climate were similar to those that the soldiers might encounter in Europe, the site was chosen as a simulated training environment. At one point 10,000 men were at the camp. During their brief stay from 1942 to 1944, they learned how to construct bridges, roads, airstrips, and canals, while picking up other wartime skills as well.

The war ended, the soldiers returned to civilian life, and everything but the officers' quarters was completely razed. The remaining structure is known as the Great Hall, and if you have visited, you know the architecture is undeniably great. With a large workforce, it took only six months to build. Most materials were locally sourced, like the massive pines used for beams and tons of lava rock used for the fireplace. Those guys had to have something to do in the middle of the forest!

After the soldiers left, the Great Hall served as a great place to store livestock. Can you imagine the smell? Renovation began when developer/owner John Gray made a deal with Hollywood to install a new roof in exchange for

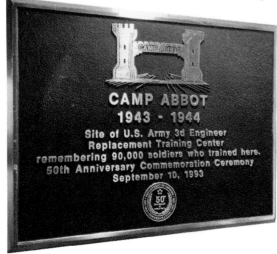

CAMP ABBOT
1943 - 1944
Site of U.S. Army 3d Engineer
Replacement Training Center
remembering 90,000 soldiers who trained here.
50th Anniversary Commemoration Ceremony
September 10, 1993

Inside the Great Hall

WORLD WAR II CAMP

WHAT: Camp Abbot (Great Hall)

WHERE: Great Hall Loop, Sunriver

COST: Free to visit the Great Hall, but very expensive to rent!

PRO TIP: If you need to rent a meeting space and really want to impress people, rent one of the many rooms at the Great Hall!

filming *The Way West*, in which the building served as Fort Bridger.

These days pics and historical info throughout the building attest to its past. The beautiful design makes it one of the most sought-after and liveliest places in Central Oregon to host weddings, parties, conventions, and such. The endless outdoor recreation and other natural wonders nearby add to its charm.

The Sunriver Nature Center & Observatory is a must-visit if you are in the area, especially for kids and amateur astronomers.

STARGAZING

Where are the best places to stargaze in Central Oregon?

A growing population in Central Oregon has brought more artificial lights. The stars become more difficult to see, but luckily, at least for the near future, we still have many places dark enough to stargaze.

The closest place in Bend is Worthy Brewing's Hopservatory. On the ground floor of the brewery, the Transporter Room has a large, 12-foot pier and walls cosmically decorated with mosaic tiles that illustrate the universe. TV monitors display facts about space. Walk upstairs to the Dome and get a stunning panorama from Mount Hood to Mount Bachelor. Thursday through Sunday evenings and sometimes during special lunar events, the Hopservatory's resident astronomer will show you the brightest objects in the sky through the powerful telescope.

A visit to Pine Mountain Observatory is mandatory for true stargazers. The mixture of elevation, clean air, and pitch-dark surroundings create perfect conditions. On weekends from Memorial Day until the end of September anyone can visit and get intimate with the cosmos. Astronomers on hand will point out the visible features of the night sky to the novice.

The Oregon Observatory in Sunriver boasts the largest collection of public telescopes in the entire United States! When they sun sets, they are available for us to gaze at the beauty and brilliance of the night sky.

A short drive away, the Badlands, the Cascade Lakes, and the many other open areas in Central Oregon all provide stellar viewing opportunities of the night sky. Wherever you decide to gaze at the stars, an endless universe awaits.

The Hopservatory at Worthy Brewing

Recently, Prineville Reservoir State Park became designated as an official international Dark Sky Area. Only 174 of these locations exist worldwide, so you can imagine this is an amazing spot to camp and view the stars on a clear night.

SNOW AND CLIMATE

It's April—will the winter ever end?

People often ask about all the rain in Oregon. They fail to realize that Oregon is a huge state, the 10th largest in the country, and has many microclimates, especially along the east and west sides of the Cascade Mountains.

Central Oregon, also known as the High Desert, is about as dry and dusty as a place can get. Our region only gets around 12 inches of rain per year (the national average is 30), and most precipitation is in the form of . . . SNOW!

For lovers of the white, fluffy stuff, there are plenty of fun activities during our long winters: skiing, snowboarding, sledding, sitting in front of warm fires, and drinking dark beers, to name a few. If those activities aren't for you, the Central Oregon climate can be quite frustrating. Days, sometimes weeks, of continuous snow and icy roads tend to linger and linger. People like me, who like to spend lots of time gardening and planting, can't wait until spring. And then, in mid-April, just when the days get warmer and we think winter has passed—BAM, another significant snow falls! I remember snow falling one time in June!

Longtime locals and those raised here are used to it. They laugh at warm-weather lovers like me. For many of us transplants, the seemingly endless winters are

SNOW, SNOW AND MORE SNOW

WHAT: Winter in Central Oregon

WHERE: The question should be *when?*

COST: Free to experience the cold weather, but it all depends on which winter activities you choose. A pass to Mount Bachelor? Need a wood stove? Wood for the stove? Snow tires? It can get expensive!

PRO TIP: Two choices to maintain sanity: (1) Pick up some activities that make winter fun. (2) Travel or migrate as much as possible during the colder months!

Top left: *Downtown Bend after a good snow.* Top right: *Snowshoeing in a nearby snowpark.* Bottom: *The Deschutes River.*

enough to make the most patient among us cry, so the honest answer to the question is, "It never truly ends!"

If you move to Central Oregon, learn to love (or at least tolerate) the cold and try to find enjoyable winter activities. Don't say I didn't warn you!

When it comes to gardening, locals have helped me with the adage, "When the snow is gone from Black Butte, then you can plant." It seems to work!

THE MIGHTY PILLAR

How did this giant pillar get here out of nowhere?

Nothing is quite as spectacular or as strange as nature. The history of Central Oregon is one of violent volcanic activity that formed caves, calderas, lava tubes, and other fascinating natural formations. One such rock formation is Stein's Pillar in the Ochoco National Forest.

The pillar has an intriguing history as well. Seemingly in the middle of nowhere, surrounded by pines, firs, and other native species, this towering formation of rhyolite ash rises 350 feet above its surroundings. The Indigenous Shoshone people believed the stone column reached to the gods. If they could scale it, surely they would be able to speak with the sun god. Many men attempted to climb the pillar only to fail and succumb to the fate of their death god, Masauu. Finally, a girl, though forbidden to attempt the climb, disobeyed the elders and secretly made the attempt. She succeeded!

The Great Spirit was very pleased. He instructed Coyote, the supreme ruler of all creatures, to form a union with the girl. From this union came the Shoshone people. It is said that the Shoshone held their women in the highest

PILLARS OF OREGON

WHAT: Stein's Pillar

WHERE: Ochoco National Forest, Prineville

COST: Forest Pass (Day and Annual passes available)

PRO TIP: The iconic Monkey Face at Smith Rock and Turkey Monster near Sweet Home are two others worth seeing (or climbing, if you're brave enough). These are sometimes referred to as the Three Pillars of Oregon.

Perhaps the most in-depth and fascinating books about the history of Central Oregon are the *Thunder Over the Ochoco* series by Gale Ontko.

A view of Stein's Pillar and beyond

esteem, perhaps more than any other tribe. Stein's Pillar remained a sacred and religious spot, and ceremonies were held at its base.

These days, the pillar is a popular climbing site, though not nearly as crowded as Monkey Face at Smith Rock. For those of us who are content viewing the pillar, a 4-mile hike out and back will lead to a pretty amazing overlook and get you close to the base of the column.

I AIN'T AFRAID OF NO GHOSTS

Are there any ghost towns in Central Oregon?

Ok, I'll admit it. Until I was practically an adult, I thought a ghost town meant that the area was haunted. It wasn't until I visited a few that I realized they were called ghost towns because once upon a time they had larger, thriving populations. The towns declined for many reasons, usually because industries such as logging or mining went bust. Perhaps a highway and especially railroads were built in another nearby city.

Records claim that Oregon has over 200 ghost towns! Central Oregon has a few, mostly outside of Deschutes County, but worth a stop on a road trip.

Millican is the closest to Bend. With only a lone store, closed since 2005 and in need of some TLC, all you need is a quick stop to view it while driving east on Highway 20 between Bend and Burns.

The town of Shaniko, right off of Highway 97, announces its existence with the large painted letters on an old building seen from afar. Once said to be the "Wool Capital of the Pacific Northwest,"

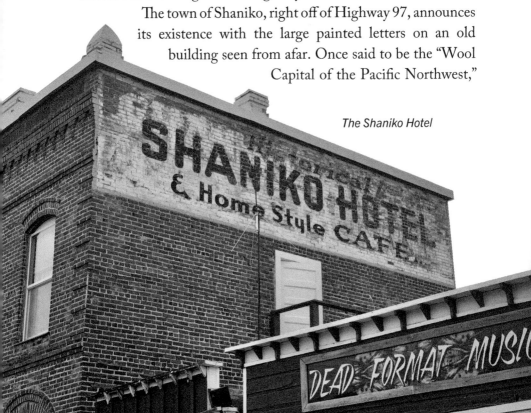

The Shaniko Hotel

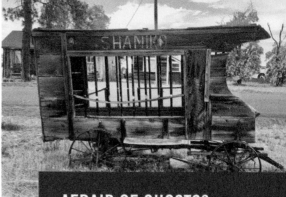

Left: *The lone building standing in Millican.* Right: *Remnants of an old wagon in Shaniko.*

many structures remain mostly intact, and perhaps one day the buildings might be restored for curious tourists.

Other off-the-beaten-track towns like Ashwood and Richmond exist (or do they?), though you might get lost even with GPS trying to find them. It depends on your sense of adventure and whether seeing a few old buildings is worth the hassle. I enjoy it, and reading a bit about the history before visiting enhances the experience.

It also seems people have different ideas of what constitutes a ghost town. Can Antelope, Oregon, be called a ghost town? For a brief period, the area's population swelled to over 7,000 when Bhagwan Shree Rajneesh brought hundreds of his followers to the area. Now the population is a mere 40 people. Read the history (or watch the Netflix documentary) of that one for some fun!

Shaniko is indeed having somewhat of a renaissance. Events are returning, and the tourists are coming!

A UNIQUE CEMETERY

Why would I want to visit a cemetery?

Cemeteries can be fascinating—the history, the tales those departed souls could tell of lives full of happiness and pain, joy and sorrow. Every one of them had a story.

The Camp Polk Cemetery near Sisters is unlike any burial ground in Central Oregon. Often called the pioneer cemetery, unconventional memorials pay respect to many of the founding settlers of the area. The gravesites have no uniformity whatsoever, and they are decorated with elaborate markers, wood carvings, a variety of stones, and a hodgepodge of other items.

Tales of an interesting and sometimes difficult past seem to come alive, especially if you register for a free tour with the Three Sister Historical Society or the Deschutes Land Trust. The guide, often dressed in frontier clothing to make the tour seem more authentic, will share the gossip and history of a time long

FRONTIER CEMETERY

WHAT: Camp Polk Reserve and Cemetery

WHERE: Cemetery Road, Sisters

COST: Free

PRO TIP: The Deschutes Land Trust does an amazing, unprecedented job of protecting lands in the county. Consider donating to the cause and scheduling other fun tours with topics like bird watching, stargazing, butterfly identification, and more. The organization is truly a blessing to conservation.

Not many more people can be buried in the Camp Polk Cemetery. Besides being small, it rests on a slope, and longtime locals have decided that only those who have direct ties to original families of the area can claim plots.

Top: *Entrance to the Camp Polk Cemetery.* Inset: *Remnants of the Hindman homestead*

gone—the first murder victim of Deschutes County, who married whom, what happened to so and so, and other juicy stories.

Camp Polk Cemetery is full of bodies and some of the most fascinating history in all of Central Oregon! In fact, the adjacent Camp Polk Reserve, cared for by the Deschutes Land Trust, was originally a Civil War-era military post where soldiers protected settlers from Indian attacks. It later became one of the first homesteads in Central Oregon.

HAIRCUTS AND BELT BUCKLES

Would you look at the size of that belt buckle?

At the L&K Barber Shop in downtown Bend, patrons get quite a treat. Not only can they get a stylish haircut, but they also get a chance to see the largest collection of belt buckles in all of Central Oregon, most likely in the entire state!

People collect everything, so why not belt buckles? As soon as you walk in the door of the shop, the specially-built glass cases along the wall, full of shiny, gleaming brass donated from customers all over the world, catch your attention.

Deer, wolves, eagles, and horses are common motifs engraved on the buckles. The American flag, beer, military service, and other themes all represent more than just something to hold your pants up. Quite a few buckles stand out for their unique colors, shapes, or other intricate designs. Many were created for the annual Sisters Rodeo. Honestly, I never realized how much craftsmanship went into creating them. They truly are pieces of art.

Perhaps the oldest barbershop in Bend, L&K was opened over 50 years ago in 1968 by Lou and Kathy Bankston (thus the L&K). The current owner, Debbie Bennett, worked there for many years before she finally purchased the shop, and she continues the unique belt-buckle tradition.

According to Roadside America, (a really fun website to use when roadtripping), the largest belt buckle can be found in Abilene, Kansas, at a whopping 19 feet 10 inches wide by 13 feet 11 inches tall!

Two of the many cases of belt buckles at the barbershop

BELT BUCKLES GALORE

WHAT: Lots and lots of really cool belt buckles

WHERE: L&K Barber Shop, 105 NW Oregon Ave.

COST: Free to view

PRO TIP: Get a haircut while there and shoot the breeze with the friendly barbers.

Barbershops are ground zero for interesting conversations, and Debbie and the other barbers always seem up for a lively chat. If the belt buckles could talk, I imagine each one would have some stories to share as well.

ASTRONAUT TRAINING

Where can I pretend to be an astronaut?

So you want to be an astronaut when you grow up? At one point, I think many of us do. Few of us will travel to space, the final frontier, but we can still pretend without ever leaving Central Oregon. In fact, real astronauts from the famous Apollo mission that first landed on the moon trained here during the 1960s!

The Newberry National Volcanic Monument encompasses over 54,000 acres of lava flows, caves, lakes, and the Newberry Crater, a caldera that is still seismically active. In other words, it could still erupt at any time!

Before anyone landed on the moon, no one knew exactly what to expect. Experts believed Newberry and the nearby McKenzie lava fields, because they are composed of basalts formed from rapidly cooling molten rock (similar to the moon), would provide a pretty good idea of what they might encounter on the mission. This part of Earth is about the closest environment we can simulate to the lunar surface or some other desolate planet that we may one day explore. For a while Central Oregon was deemed Moon Country.

THE MOON ON EARTH

WHAT: Newberry National Volcanic Monument

WHERE: 58201 S Hwy. 97

COST: $5 day-use pass, $30 annual

PRO TIP: Some highlights of the area (like the Lava River Cave) are not open year-round. Be sure to research before a visit.

Taking rocks or other materials from national parks and monuments is prohibited. However, Oregon State Parks allow rockhounding on a smaller level. Be sure to ask!

When visiting, it is easy to see why. Hikes through the Lava Cast Forest, the Trail of Molten Land, the Big Obsidian Flow, and others lead through jagged pieces of lava rock ranging from basalt to rhyolite. On a sunny day, the heat radiates off the dark rock. Though it's doubtful that anyone would want to suit up in an astronaut's outfit, exploring the landscape definitely creates an otherworldly experience.

Top and center: *Lava River Cave.* Bottom: *View of the Lava Fields.*

THIS LAND IS YOUR LAND, THIS LAND IS MY LAND

Why is there so much public land in Central Oregon?

In many states, most property is privately owned, but there's a surprising amount of public land in Oregon. In fact, do you realize the government owns over half of Oregon?

Yep, Oregon ranks fifth among US states with about 53 percent of its land owned by the federal, state or local government. Nevada ranks first with just over 80 percent. Crazy, huh? Deschutes County is actually second out of Oregon counties with just over 77 percent.

Obviously, the West was not settled as quickly as the East. Not only was the trek over the mountain ranges treacherous, but much of the land is uninhabitable, or at least not ideal for farming or creating a viable livelihood.

Gold rushes, railroads, and large tracts of land given through federal incentives like the homesteading acts brought settlers west for what they believed to be a better life. Often lured deceitfully, they tried to green the deserts, but only the toughest remained and thrived. Many of those became cattlemen and sheepherders.

Explore tiny forest roads on public lands, especially those not listed on maps. So much to discover. You'll feel like a modern-day explorer.

The Badlands of Central Oregon

YOUR LAND, MY LAND

WHAT: The public lands of Oregon

WHERE: All around us!

COST: Inexpensive permits for day use or overnighting

PRO TIP: Join or volunteer with a local conservation group like Deschutes Land Trust, Oregon Natural Desert Association (ONDA), Central Oregon LandWatch, and others to help protect the land for future generations.

Much of the land went unclaimed or ownership reverted back to the government. Over the years notable conservation groups and individuals like former Oregon Governor Tim McCall waged successful battles to protect the land and maintain it for public use.

The Deschutes and Ochoco National Forest, the Mount Jefferson and Three Sisters Wilderness, and other lands comprise much of Central Oregon. Great for everyone, because nowadays we get to hike, bike, camp, and recreate in the majority of this open space. Debates often arise about its most beneficial use, the effect on housing prices, how to deal with fire management, and other issues. But one thing is certain: You'll be grateful for the opportunity to get out there and forest bathe in all the beautiful nature that is literally in our backyard.

DEE WRIGHT OBSERVATORY

What is that really awesome tower made of lava?

Along an old wagon road that is now the scenic McKenzie Pass, visitors get the chance to see what might be the most awesome observation tower ever built.

Forged completely from black lava stone, the Dee Wright Observatory stands out majestically in contrast to a usually blue sky. The structure was built during the Great Depression with a crew led by Dee Wright, a longtime trail builder and respected park service employee. Unfortunately, Wright did not live to see completion, but his name lives on with the tower for the foreseeable future.

At 5,187 feet, the observatory offers a panoramic view that rivals any other in Central Oregon. Strategically placed windows on the bottom level each offer a view of a different mountain peak. At the top, a 360-degree peak finder lists the buttes, craters, and mountains in the distance. On a clear day the naked eye can see Mount Jefferson, the Three Sisters, and as far as Mount Hood. Even Collier Glacier on North Sister, the largest in Central Oregon, is visible if the snow has not completely melted!

Nearby, a short, half-mile interpretive trail meanders through the seemingly endless lava fields that surround the observatory. Summer, though hot with the radiating black rock, is a good time to visit, though autumn right before the snow falls might be cooler. Snow covers the highway much of the year, and the road is closed.

TOWER OF LAVA

WHAT: Dee Wright Observatory

WHERE: McKenzie Highway

COST: Free

PRO TIP: Take a day trip (or more) and drive the 82-mile McKenzie Highway-Santiam Pass Scenic Highway. Though the Dee Wright Observatory is the highlight in my opinion, there is much more to explore.

Top left: *Inside the observatory.*
Top right: *View from inside the observatory.* Inset: *View of the entire observatory from the road.*

As mentioned in an earlier entry, this area is another spot where astronauts trained. You'll have an otherworldly experience when visiting!

When the cumulus clouds dot the blue sky and contrast against the black lava rock, this place makes for some of the most amazing pictures in all of Oregon!

INDIGENOUS PEOPLE

Who were the first people to inhabit this area?

A recent discovery near the town of Riley, Oregon, suggests that one the oldest human civilizations on our continent was right here in our state. Archeologists uncovered two scrapers (human-made tools) thought to be over 18,000 years old!

Our knowledge of those ancient cultures does not go back that far, but we know that before Europeans, Indigenous tribes thrived throughout the state, including the High Desert. Though an inhospitable environment, they survived on native vegetation such as cama roots, hunted roaming deer and elk, and enjoyed the abundant fish in the rivers, lakes, and streams. Like the indigenous people from other parts of the country, local tribes were eventually forced onto reservations. In Central Oregon the Warm Springs Reservation became home to a confederation of three tribes—The Paiute, Wasco, and the Warm Springs.

Today, the reservation is over 640,000 acres. It is self-governed, and the tribes have their own constitution. Educational programs attempt to preserve and protect their cultural

OREGON'S FIRST INHABITANTS

WHAT: The Museum at Warm Springs

WHERE: 2189 Hwy. 96, Warm Springs

COST: $7 for adults as of this writing

PRO TIP: For an enhanced visit to the Museum at Warm Springs, plan your visit on a day when a tribal event is taking place.

Thunder over the Ochocos by Gale Ontko might be the most in-depth account of Central Oregon history dating back to pre-European days. Worth a read for true history buffs!

Top left and right. *Exhibits inside the Warm Springs Museum. Bottom: A walk along the water near the museum.*

heritage—languages, skills, customs, and more. Businesses like the Indian Head Casino and the Kah-Nee-Ta Resort help economically.

A short entry here is not enough to do their history and culture justice, but there are numerous books about each tribe. Better yet, the Museum at Warm Spring has a wealth of information and is the most interactive way to learn. The High Desert Museum has ongoing exhibits worth visiting as well.

COLD, COOL CAVES

Did Bend really used to get its ice from caves?

Caves have been explored and used by humans as long as we have existed. In Oregon, stories abound about how people stumbled upon many of them unintentionally and then put them to use. Over 1,000 caves have been mapped in the state so far, and some don't even have names yet!

The most visited in our area is the Lava River Cave, the longest in Oregon at just over a mile. Located at Newberry National Monument, the cave closes from October to May to protect the bat population, but otherwise it is the most popular and easiest to access. Skeleton, the Redmond Caves (mentioned earlier), Skylight, and Boyd are just a few of the other popular ones that adventurous spelunkers can visit on their own.

Caves have more practical uses than many realize. During a time before refrigerators, food could be preserved longer when stored in these dark, chilly caverns. In fact, ice from Arnold Ice Cave was delivered to Bend on a regular basis. Can you imagine? Quite the entrepreneurial endeavor!

Different types of entrepreneurs known as moonshiners also used these hidden earthen cavities to concoct spirits during Prohibition. Moonshine Cave derives its name from an abandoned distillery found there, and some say there still might be equipment inside the lesser-known caves. It's hard to believe that Oregon, today known for its numerous breweries and wineries, was dry once upon a time. Or it was supposed to be, at any rate.

Speaking of caves and such, the world's oldest known human footwear was found at Fort Rock Cave right here in Central Oregon!

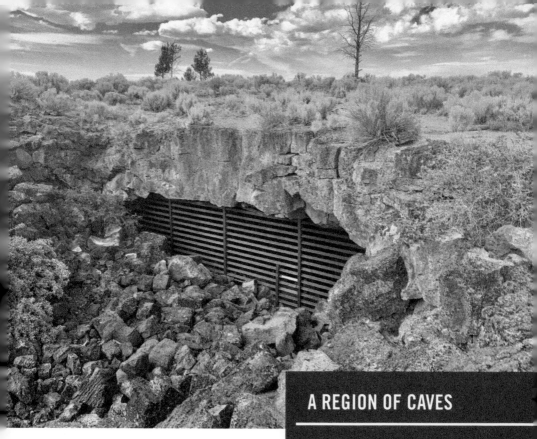

Some caves, like this one, are closed to the public.

A REGION OF CAVES

WHAT: Central Oregon caves

WHERE: All around Central Oregon

COST: Lava River Cave costs, but most are free to explore. Some are closed, and some are on private land. Research before you go.

PRO TIP: Bring flashlights, a jacket (it can be cold inside the caves!), and a friend.

Shelters, hideouts, makeout spots, canvases for the less intelligent among us to graffiti with modern day hieroglyphics—caves still have many purposes today. Wanderlust Tours even has an a capella group perform live music inside one every year! There remain undiscovered (or at least unmapped) caves, and we always seem to be creating new ways to use these earthly wonders. What would you do with your own cave?

ATTENTION ALL PILOTS!

Is there an airport in the middle of a neighborhood near Pilot Butte?

We all know about Central Oregon's largest airport in Redmond (RDM), which the majority of us use for our travels. Most people are aware of the smaller Bend Municipal Airport (KBDN). Interestingly enough, KBDN is home to a flight training school, businesses, and noncommercial aircraft. And here's a fun fact. It's the third largest in Oregon in terms of takeoffs and landings, with only the Portland (PDX) and Hillsboro (HIO) airports claiming more traffic!

Much like devoted golfers who desire a home on or near a golf course, the small Pilot Butte Airport (8OR5) became the fulfilled dream of some local aviation enthusiasts. They got together and in the 1960s built the Aerospace Acres residential neighborhood on what was then the outskirts of Bend. As the city grew, other neighborhoods built up around it, but since they were there first, they got to stay. It's doubtful this would be permitted today, but according to the managers, they have never had issues and have always maintained an amicable relationship with the city. In fact, they often meet with officials and planners to make sure future construction will not interfere with the airport. The pilots make every effort to respect the neighbors and keep flights limited to daytime hours.

Nine residents currently share the airstrip and all of them own homes (the requirement for using the completely private airstrip and hangars). Unfortunately, if readers are hoping to use the Pilot Butte Airport you will have to wait until an owner sells. Since this is very uncommon, it might be a long wait.

The landing strip

NEIGHBORHOOD AIRPORT

WHAT: Pilot Butte Airport

WHERE: 1928 S Cooper Pl.

COST: Free to view, but if you want to use it, get to know a pilot or buy a home!

PRO TIP: The nearby Larkspur Trail is one of the most unique urban trails in Bend. Hike it to see for yourself.

The airstrip is easily visible from the busy Bear Creek Road. Two streets with the names of Cessna Drive and Airstrip Drive make the area easy to find. Not far from part of the Larkspur Trail a small path leads to a chain-link fence with a foreboding NO TRESPASSING sign. At least a few hangars and a veritable runway are visible, and two thoughts immediately come to mind. "How in the world does someone land a plane on such a small patch of land?" and "How cool is this?"

WHOLE IN THE WALL

What's so cool about the tiny town of Mitchell, Oregon?

More than the hot spots, the crowded trails, and the overrun restaurants, it's those less-visited places that really catch my interest. The tiny town of Mitchell, Oregon, is such a place. Nestled on a hill about an hour west of Prineville on Highway 26, blink and you might drive right past without even noticing it.

Perhaps the last significant town before we reach what is no longer considered Central Oregon, Mitchell boasts the moniker "Gateway to the Painted Hills," part of the John Day Fossil Beds National Monument (another spot worth visiting and mentioned in this book).

Founded in 1873, Mitchell became a waypoint for ranchers, miners, and logging men. They earned it a rough-and-tumble reputation, and it became infamous as "Tiger Town." At its peak, Main Street, a small strip running

MITCHELL, OREGON

WHAT: The tiny town of Mitchell

WHERE: Mitchell

COST: Free to visit

PRO TIP: If you're a hot wing or beer fan, visit Tiger Town, the coolest brewery in Central Oregon! You will not be disappointed.

A long standing remnant of Mitchell's past, the Whole in the Wall

through town, had five saloons and a house of ill repute. The town's most popular current resident, Tiger Town Brewery, is named after this rowdy history.

These days a drive down Main Street offers a glimpse of the past. Old buildings like the Oregon Hotel (more than 100 years old), the Wheeler County Trading Company, and a few others are still open for business and thriving. Others, like the Whole in the Wall, are waiting for a new owner to revive them. You won't see many homes or neighborhoods along the strip because most residents live out of sight farther up "Piety Hill."

Some might call Mitchell a ghost town. The ups and downs of local economies have all contributed to its current state, but at one point the population reached over 400, twice the number of people it has today! Yet, no matter the number of people, it still teems with life and energy. Though growing, Mitchell is unlikely to become a big city anytime soon. The locals are totally OK with that.

Located near Mitchell is the Shoe Tree (actually, it appears to be multiple trees), where many people have left their best sneakers and footwear in hopes they will become rich, famous, or whatever their hearts desire. Make a wish!

WATER IS LIFE

What river runs through Bend?

OK, it's common knowledge the Deschutes River runs through Bend. Even small children and tourists learn this fact quickly enough. But what do you really know about the importance of the area's most prized resource?

More than just an amazing spot to float on a hot summer day, the Deschutes River is the lifeblood of the area. A major tributary of the Columbia River, its headwaters begin at Little Lava Lake in the Cascades. Before reaching the Columbia, it flows south to north through towns like Bend, Warm Springs, Maupin, and a few others.

The French explorers called it Des Chutes, meaning "of the falls" and referring to the many waterfalls and rapids. It was once a major obstacle for those along the Oregon Trail, and entire towns popped up thanks to industrious individuals who decided to set up river crossings.

Native species of trout and countless other wildlife depend on these waters, as did the Indigenous people and early settlers who lived

LIFEBLOOD OF A REGION

WHAT: The Deschutes River

WHERE: Begins at Little Lava Lake and flows into the Columbia River

COST: Priceless

PRO TIP: You don't have to be an ecologist to help the Deschutes! Learn more about the river by joining or reading about organizations such as the Deschutes River Conservancy and the Deschutes River Alliance.

Want to whitewater raft the Deschutes? The small town of Maupin offers some of the best whitewater trips on the river.

The amazingly beautiful Deschutes River

nearby. Irrigation of the river has been and still is responsible for the livelihood of farmers, and in fact, the development of the entire area!

The lumber mills used the Deschutes as an automatic conveyor of sorts to transport and store large logs. Photos of what the Old Mill area looked like 50 years ago show that the difference in its appearance today is astounding.

Next time you're picnicking, paddleboarding, fishing, or engaging in some other activity that involves use of the river, watch the flowing water and appreciate its significance. More than recreation, the Deschutes River is the soul of Central Oregon. Respect and care for it.

ILLEGAL BUT FUN!

Are there any speakeasies in Bend?

Once upon a time, during Prohibition, illicit hangout spots called speakeasies popped up in cities all around the United States. People had to have their alcohol, and the social aspect of drinking with others was just as important, if not more so.

Obviously, a true speakeasy has no reason to exist these days (unless you are trying to avoid permits or selling your own homebrews), but often businesses like to recreate the historical, forbidden vibe of those days.

Central Oregon has a few places that have been intentionally set up like speakeasies. McMenamins' secret rooms were discussed in a previous entry. Their Broom Closet, a well-hidden room on the top floor of the Art House building, awaits with cocktails and other spirits. Cellar 65, the newest spot as of this writing, is located under the Blissful Spoon. Art on the dark walls depicts women in 1920s-style clothing. Domaine Serene, the downtown wine bar, also boasts an underground basement turned drinking establishment.

Backside Kegs has a more modern-day speakeasy concept. It's a local hangout with lots of beers on tap, and the big-screen TVs make it a great place for watching sports or playing a game of ping pong and foosball. Were those games a thing 100 years ago?

Want a few more? San Simon and The Cellar, both in downtown Bend, have eclectic speakeasy vibes, though they're perhaps not intentionally set up like the one at Seventh Mountain Resort. There, the designer went all out at the Outfitter Bar to create a secret room with gangster photos and period-designed furniture.

The hidden speakeasy at Gompers Distillery

PROHIBITION ERA FUN

WHAT: Speakeasies

WHERE: Various locations in Central Oregon

COST: Free admission, but $$ to drink

PRO TIP: Each of the spots has its own unique vibe. Find your favorite!

Perhaps lesser known, but maybe the closest to a genuine speakeasy, is a small room at Gompers Distillery in Redmond. It's superbly hidden, and no one would ever find it unless shown or if they have x-ray vision. An old record player, wallpaper, pictures, and furniture all match the Prohibition era. It's usually used only for private parties and members, but if you ask nicely they might let you take a peek or enjoy a beverage inside the room.

Exploring these locations should keep you busy for a while, and if the popular trend continues, we will probably see more of them pop up, which would be OK with me!

REJUVENATING HOT SPRINGS

What is the most ideal way to stay warm in winter?

When the winter weather hits we search for ways to warm our bodies: wood stoves, warming fires, layers of clothing, hot chocolate. Not all of us own or have easy access to a hot tub. And even if we do, nothing is as gratifying as soaking in the waters of natural pools and hot springs.

Luckily, Oregon has lots of options. In Bend, McMenamins is the closest spot to warm your bones. The popular location downtown boasts a large, Turkish-style hot pool. Beautifully crafted stained glass windows depict the sun, the moon, and St. Francis's compassion for animals. The shimmering turquoise tiles give the pool an opulent air. Add the fountain, water-spouting lions, and an open ceiling and the soaker feels like royalty.

Near Bend, yet undeveloped, are the natural hot springs at East Lake and Paulina Lake located in the Newberry Caldera. On the south lake shore of East Lake, soakers can find a pool of magma-heated water ranging from 104 to 120 degrees! The north shore of Paulina Lake also has small pools dug by volunteers. Whether these pools are usable depends completely on the water level. By late fall or winter, the lakes are usually high, and the springs might be submerged.

Those might be the only ones in Central Oregon, but being located smack dab in the middle of the state has its advantages. Short road

WINTER WARMTH

WHAT: Refreshing, natural hot springs

WHERE: Central Oregon and a bit beyond

COST: Prices vary, from really cheap (free) like Paulina Lake to really expensive (but worth it) like Breitenbush.

PRO TIP: Many of these spots are considered "clothing optional," so bring your birthday suit!

Top: *Terwilliger (Cougar) Hot Springs.*
Inset: *Crane Hot Springs.*

trips in all directions lead to well-known hot springs like Belknap Hot
Springs Gardens & Lodge or Terwilliger Hot Springs in the Willamette
Valley. Breitenbush, one of the more luxurious experiences, is only a two-
hour drive north of Bend. Going east, Crane Hot Springs is near Burns.
Southeast is Summer Lake, located in the Oregon Outback. Who says
there aren't reasons to get excited about winter?!

We might have an addition to the list by the
time of publication. After being closed since
2018, the famed Kah Nee Ta Resort in Warm
Springs plans to reopen and will include both
hot springs and a water park.

WHAT'S UP, GNOMIE?

All these beer festivals! If I had to pick one, which would it be?

Who says you have to pick one? Why not write a long list (a few pages probably) of all the beer celebrations in Central Oregon and go to every single one?

OK, perhaps you're not a raging alcoholic but you do want the most unique experience. In my opinion, The Little Woody Barrel-Aged Beer, Cider & Whiskey Festival is the coolest and most original of them all.

During the festival, true beer aficionados celebrate brews and whiskeys from Oregon breweries and distilleries. I say true fans because these drinks have unique flavors not often available at the pubs or in stores. Brewers age specialty beers using old barrels, usually oak, that once contained whiskey, wine, rum, and other spirits (or even ingredients like maple syrup). The taste depends on your palate; some flavors work and some don't. Still, the process takes time, patience, and ingenuity to create them, so I'm willing to be the guinea pig. Why let all their hard work go to waste?

Upon admission everyone gets a small taster glass, and festival-goers use little wooden tokens to purchase samples. Some claim the samples are generous, but I always appreciate more for my money. Still, many of these brews have high ABV (alcohol by volume) so best

At dusk you can watch the Vaux's swifts fly down the chimney across the street at the historic Boys and Girls Club building. It's pretty freaking cool.

124

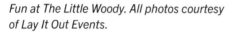

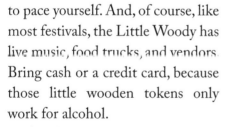

Fun at The Little Woody. All photos courtesy of Lay It Out Events.

to pace yourself. And, of course, like most festivals, the Little Woody has live music, food trucks, and vendors. Bring cash or a credit card, because those little wooden tokens only work for alcohol.

Another reason to like this festival is because it's held on the lawn of Deschutes Historical Museum. Some of the proceeds are donated to the museum as well. And the best part? The folks running around inebriated and dressed as gnomes of course!

BEERS & GNOMES

WHAT: The Little Woody Beer & Whiskey Festival

WHERE: Deschutes Historical Museum

COST: $20 to $45

PRO TIP: Dress up as a gnome and you might get extra wooden tokens!

WATCH OUT FOR THE FIRE!

Can I really camp out in a real fire lookout?

Yep! Camping out in a real fire lookout is possible, but only if you can get a reservation. Renting one of these spots overnight is tougher than scoring Taylor Swift tickets! And honestly, I'd much rather camp in a tower overlooking the beauty of the wilderness any day.

Oregon has thousands of acres of national forest, which also brings the inevitable possibility of fires. For over a century, the US Forest Service has manned thousands of these fire lookouts across the country. Technology such as infrared images, satellites, and solar-powered drones have all but replaced most lookouts. Some are still used for their original purpose, but many are defunct to the point where only pieces of wood or metal remnants remain.

When the intact towers are not in use by fire watchers, lucky folks have the opportunity to rent them and experience a remote, peaceful evening surrounded by forest. Imagine the unimpeded night sky, the howling coyotes, and the low hum of insects.

Closest to Bend is the Green Ridge Lookout. At only $40 a night, it's a steal, and the rental fees for stays in all of these towers go toward preserving the structures. Hager Mountain, Gold Butte, and Indian Ridge are some others available for rent in or near Central Oregon. At last count, recreation.gov lists 17 total in the state. All the towers have short windows during the year for lodging. Even if you can't get a coveted reservation, the hikes leading to them are still amazing.

Recreation.com has streamlined the camping and permit process over the past few years. This site is where you will find reservations for the lookouts, camping and more.

View from atop of Maxwell Butte

NO FIRES HERE

WHAT: Fire Lookout Towers

WHERE: 17 available in Oregon for rentals!

COST: Prices vary by tower, but you only need a day pass or permit to hike and see them.

PRO TIP: Get your coffee brewing and get up super early to wait on the computer for the permits to go live. Hey, it might work.

LITTLE RANGERS

Can my kid really become a ranger?

Ready for your child to get a job and help pay for groceries? What do you mean she's too young?

Seriously though, parents who visit the US National Parks might be aware of the Junior Ranger program offered for kids. It's a super-cool way to learn, plus you get to collect badges. When kids get to a park they can pick up a booklet, usually at the visitor center, and complete a variety of activities depending on the location—there are questions about the local fauna, flora, and landscape; crossword puzzles and word searches; scavenger hunts; and more. Some badges require kids to attend an in-person ranger talk or a hands-on activity. These are the most fun and exciting. After the required activities are completed, return to the visitor center and repeat a pledge to become an official ranger and get a free badge!

When my daughters are working through the booklets, I often learn along with them. Honestly, I've earned a few badges of my own as an adult. I'm not sure if it was technically allowed, but the ranger knew I was a kid at heart. Besides, have you ever met a ranger who wasn't friendly? Not me!

Some state parks also offer the Junior Ranger program. When you visit, stop by a ranger station or visitors center and ask.

The author's daughters, Sofi and Kaia, reciting the Junior Ranger Pledge!

Nearest Bend, the Newberry National Monument has the Junior Ranger program. Kids learn about volcanic activity in the region, identify various rocks, and get a lesson in life science among other things. Crater Lake, Oregon's only national park, also offers a book where young rangers can create their own park, help protect the wildlife, and learn the history of Mount Mazama.

According to the National Park Service, over 200 badges can be earned. Many of them are unique, some are made of wood and others of plastic, and they often come in different shapes. They all display the name of each national park. Most importantly, it's an outstanding way to learn a ton about our country and the environment.

QUILTS, QUILTS, AND MORE QUILTS!

Where can I get a quilt to keep me warm during these cold winters?

Well, it just so happens that the small town of Sisters mentioned previously in this book has one of the largest quilt shows in the country and the largest outdoor quilt show in the entire world!

Founded way back in 1975, the Sisters Outdoor Quilt Show (SOQS) takes place on the second Saturday of July. During "Quilt Week" hundreds of these vibrant, woven fabrics are on display throughout town, and participants interested in picking up a new hobby can take classes or attend workshops. Each year has a new theme, such as Community or Renewal. Categories like Best of Show, the Block Challenge, and Wish Card make for a friendly competition among quilters who want to display their talents.

Undoubtedly, creating such stunning pieces requires time, patience, and skill. The attention to detail, decorative patterns, vivid colors, and unique motifs are astounding. Viewers cannot help but to instantly develop an appreciation for these true works of art.

My grandmother quilted, and in fact, I still have at least a few of her creations. Honestly, they are among my most prized possessions, and I plan to bequeath them to my daughters. I recall the many hours she spent, often with friends or family, quilting away and loving every minute of it. Sometimes it was a social event and other times her way of relaxing.

Many of the remarkable quilts at the SOQS are for sale and are very reasonably priced, especially considering the amount of time

---

The International Quilt Show in Houston, Texas, is said to be the largest quilt show in the United States!

An up close shot of a colorful quilt at the Stitchin' Post

the quilters spent making them. Whether used to keep warm on a chilly Central Oregon evening or for a wall or bed decoration, they will certainly add character and comfort to your home.

QUILT MANIA

WHAT: Sisters Outdoor Quilt Show

WHERE: Sisters

COST: Free

PRO TIP: Can't make it the SOQS? Stop by the Stitchin' Post while in Sisters to view or purchase quilts and everything else you need to pick up the hobby on your own!

BALANCING ROCKS

How in the world do those rocks not fall?

The Metolius River is well known for its beauty, world-class trout fishing, hiking, and the numerous other activities along its banks. It's a favorite spot for my family to have picnics and relax on a sunny day.

Emerging from two natural springs in the Deschutes National Forest near Black Butte, the river flows north into Lake Billy Chinook. On warm days, boaters and water enthusiasts galore descend on this lake located in the scenic Cove Palisades State Park.

With so many things to do around the river and lake, lesser-known natural spectacles in the park often go unseen. The Metolius Balancing Rocks are one such spectacle.

Time and Central Oregon's violent volcanic past formed these structures. Erosion wore away the softer, bottom tuff (a type of rock created from spewing volcanic ash) leaving larger boulders that defy gravity as they sit precariously atop long, thin, worn spires. Quite the oddity of nature, they look as if they could fall at any moment!

These hoodoos were almost hidden until a fire blazed through an overgrown juniper forest in 2002. Since then, the state has created a short trail and signage that leads to an overlook. In the backdrop both Lake Billy Chinook and the prominent Mount Jefferson are visible, adding to an already stunning view. Honestly, the beautiful drive through Cove Palisades State Park is reason enough to visit. The Metolius Balancing Rocks are an extra treat and an ode to the weirdness of nature.

BALANCING ACT

WHAT: The Metolius Balancing Rocks

WHERE: Cove Palisades State Park, Culver

COST: Free

PRO TIP: The Crooked River Petroglyph is another fascinating site in the park that often gets overlooked. Supposedly carved by local tribes who once inhabited the area, it can be seen on a 20-ton boulder located across from the park headquarters.

Lake Billy Chinook is the confluence for three of Oregon's most important rivers—the Metolius, the Deschutes, and the Crooked River.

Top: *View from the Metolius Balancing Rock Trail.* Bottom: *One of the balancing rocks*

CHRISTMAS TREE, O CHRISTMAS TREE

Where can I find the best Christmas tree in Central Oregon?

Forests galore surround us. As we take those scenic drives, especially near the holiday season, it seems every other tree looks like that perfect Christmas tree. If only we could cut one down.

Guess what? We can!

But wait—not so fast!

The National Forest Service provides guidelines and specific spots to hunt for trees located on public land. The guidelines are mostly common sense, but many people these days need to be reminded. For example, do not cut trees on private land, near highways, within 300 feet of bodies of water, or in wilderness areas. Cut the entire tree, not just the top. If it's taller than 12 feet, let the old fella live and leave it alone! Bring proper tools like a handsaw or hatchet; dress for the cold weather; pack snacks and water, and possibly some snowshoes and emergency items for an adventure deep into the woods. You know, all the basic stuff.

If pine trees are your preference, they can be found at lower elevations near Bend. Those majestic firs and strong-scented cedars we usually associate with Christmas are found at higher altitudes, for example, in the Sisters area.

Most importantly, please don't be one of those entitled people who mess it up for everyone. Instead, follow these simple guidelines

---

Not many places in our country are surrounded by evergreen forests like Central Oregon. The perfect tree is nearby awaiting a new home. Make it a tradition!

#Lokipup got a new toy for Christmas.

so the generations after us (your kids, grandkids, and beyond) can enjoy the tradition. When in doubt, don't cut. Or at the very least, look up Christmas tree permits on recreation.gov for more recommendations. Keep the forests beautiful, people!

FREE TREES

WHAT: Christmas trees (and other native vegetation)

WHERE: Designated parts of Central Oregon

COST: Get a permit. It is much cheaper than a tree from Michigan at Home Depot or Lowe's!

PRO TIP: Other types of native species can be dug up to be planted in your yard as well. Natives almost always do better and thrive.

DIGGING FOR FOSSILS

Can I really dig for fossils in Oregon?

Any paleontologists in the family? If so, living in Central Oregon is a dream come true. First, take a trip to the John Day Fossil Bed National Monument. The monument consists of three separate units: Sheep Rock, Clarno, and the Painted Hills. Distinctive hikes in all of them tell the story of the past through millions of years of layered soils and rock formations.

The Thomas Condon Visitor Center at the Sheep Rock Unit has a museum where you can watch an orientation film, view murals that depict the ancient environment, and see hundreds of authentic fossil specimens on display. Get there at the right time and you might see real paleontologists in the working lab. With over 60,000 specimens dating back millions of years, they have plenty to study. Visitors leave with a wealth of information, but because John Day has national monument status, the area is protected. Sorry, no digging.

ANCIENT RELICS

WHAT: Digging for fossils

WHERE: Fossil (and learning about and viewing fossils at John Day Fossil Beds)

COST: Starting at $3 for groups, $5 for individuals

PRO TIP: Dinosaur National Park in Colorado might be one of the most underrated national parks in the country. Not only is the scenery spectacular, but witnessing the ancient history through dinosaur remains is mesmerizing and humbling.

The entrance to the Fossil Beds at Wheeler High School

John Day Fossil Beds Clarno Unit

I'm not here to tease you though. You absolutely can dig for fossils in Oregon.

Where? In the town of Fossil, of course!

Behind the spot where Wheeler High School (the only one in this town of less than 500) now stands, a lakebed existed around 33 million years ago. The property was once the ranch of Thomas Benton Hoover. When he found fossils in a claylike formation on this property, he gave the town a name that stuck.

Eventually, the area was opened to the public with plentiful fossils for the taking! These days anyone can bring shovels, gloves, eyewear, and whatever other gear they need to search for these remnants from the past. Go home with the ancient ancestors of trees, or if lucky, coveted and hard to find aquatic vertebrate fish or salamanders. Not sure what you found? The nearby Oregon Paleo Lands Center & Gallery will help identify your discoveries.

Rockhounding is also a big deal in Oregon. Those willing to dig and get dirty can find agate, thundereggs, obsidian, and other cool rocks at sites all over the state. Get a rockhounding map at Visit Bend, the local visitor center, for more details and specific locations.

HAUNTED BEND

Are there any haunted places in Bend?

Apparently, there are a number of haunted buildings in downtown Bend. The legends behind them are quite disturbing if you believe them. Even if you don't, some entertaining history can be learned on the Historical Haunts Tours offered by the Deschutes Historical Museum.

Given in early October, the walking tours are spooky and fun. Expect creepy stories about some of downtown's oldest buildings, including the first fire hall. The building later became an Italian restaurant, and a waitress claims she saw a man sitting in front of the fireplace where the firemen used to warm their bones. He reeked of woodsmoke, yet no fire was burning. As he quietly sat, he never ordered anything. When she needed the table for a larger party he had disappeared. Later the waitress saw an old photo of the fire hall in the early days. The uniforms of the crew looked just like the clothing the man had been wearing!

On to more buildings we hear about the renovation of St. Francis

SPOOKY HISTORY

WHAT: Historical Haunt Tours of Downtown Bend Walking Tours

WHERE: Deschutes Historical Museum, 129 NW Idaho Ave.

COST: $20

PRO TIP: Bundle up (it gets cold this time of year) and make plans to go at night, when it's a little more eerie.

In Redmond, a woman apparition is rumored to haunt the Redmond Hotel. Plus, the city has really freaky and fun haunted houses during the Halloween season at the Scaregrounds!

Top and bottom left: *Tour Guides share scary stories on a tour.* Right: *The Tower Theatre has a ghost or two. All photos courtesy of Deschutes Historical Museum.*

School to McMenamins, where workers reported prank pulling spirits moving objects around on their own. To this day, guests sometimes report the sound of children running around!

The most tragic tale involves infidelity and the suicide of well-established Bend proprietor William P. Downing. They say he still haunts the Downing Building to this day.

No more info—my lips are sealed, and I'm past the word limit. Better to go on a tour and hear the experts tell the full, creepy tales of these and other locations. The tours last about an hour. Fair warning. Afterward, you might need an escort back to your car if it's dark. Downtown won't seem the same anymore.

MINING FOR GOLD!

Was gold mining a thing in Central Oregon?

People are always hatching get rich quick schemes. One reason the West populated so quickly was the large waves of prospectors who were certain they would become wealthy finding gold. California and Nevada were the hot spots, but as it turned out, Baker and Grant counties were the areas in Oregon where prospectors were most likely to find the precious metal. In our part of the state most dreams ended in disappointment because the gold rush didn't pay off here like it did elsewhere.

Poor fellas, at least they tried, and a few were successful when gold was discovered in the Ochocos in 1871. Unfortunately, it was a short burst of activity. Over time, other materials proved to be lucrative, such as cinnabar, the mineral from which mercury is extracted.

For the history buff, the Ochoco Mining Ruins near Prineville sit derelict but ready to explore. Two dilapidated mercury mines, the Motherlode and Independent Mine, can be easily accessed with a short hike, although the full 7- to 8-mile hike to Lookout Mountain is more rewarding. The nearby Blue Ridge Mine also has several abandoned buildings. All three sites offer a small glimpse into past mining life, from the kilns and pipes used to extract the

GET RICH QUICK!

WHAT: The Ochoco Mining Ruins

WHERE: Ochoco National Forest

COST: Free

PRO TIP: Careful when exploring the ruins. Rusty nails, hidden critters, and falling debris can be dangerous, not to mention the mercury!

There are still many active mines in Oregon. Harney County has the most, with over 20, the majority of them basalt and cinnabar mines.

The Ochoco Mining Ruins

mercury to bunkhouses where the miners stayed during their days of backbreaking labor.

These days the remains of broken-down machinery, rotted wood, and rusty nails serve as a sanctuary for forest animals to carve out homes. Vegetation grows through every crack as the forest slowly reclaims its territory. Perhaps in a generation or two all signs of mining will be hidden and overgrown. Better check it out while you can!

EASY TRAILS

I'm not much of a hiker. Are there any trails I can drive?

Who says you have to hike to the summit of South Sister to be a true trekker? Sure, the scenery is spectacular, and the exercise does the body good, but not everybody likes to hike, plain and simple. My teenage daughters, for instance!

Sometimes you may want to cover long distances in a shorter time. Bicycles prove useful to traverse some trails, but for others, a vehicle is the best bet. Central Oregon has some of these self-guided, paved trails for autos (often called byways).

Cascade Lakes Scenic Byway starts in Bend and passes 66 miles through arguably some of the most beautiful scenery in our entire country. Along the way drivers get a taste of mountain views, pristine alpine forests, and clear lakes. A quick jaunt from the car gets you to every outdoor activity imaginable, including kayaking, swimming, camping, and boating. If it can be done outside, most likely it can be done on this route.

Foodies, beer and wine lovers, or the gardener and permaculturalist can dive deeper into the region's agricultural roots on the High Desert Food Trail. This self-guided route lists at least 45 local farms, ranches, restaurants, markets, craft and beverage makers, and more. The route

The amazingly beautiful Green Lakes Trail (not drivable)

takes shopping locally to a whole new level with fresh fruits and veggies, eggs, breads, meats, wines, whiskeys, beers . . . the list goes on! Did I mention the amazing scenery along the way?

Finally, the Newberry Country Trail (as the citizens of La Pine named it) includes some of the most unique stops in Central Oregon. It traverses crater to crater (Crater Lake to Newberry), goes east as far as Fort Rock and Christmas Valley, visits Big Red in La Pine State Park, and covers everything in between. Needless to say, don't try to do all three of these in a single day!

Seriously, take turns driving. These drives are so scenic and beautiful that it is easy to become distracted. Make plenty of stops as well to enjoy the fresh air and appreciate the beauty.

UNDERGROUND BEND

Does Bend have an underground?

In the early days of their history, Oregon cities such as Portland, Pendleton, and Astoria built a network of underground tunnels. They were used to transport goods and to avoid the busy streets above ground. They also were used for more nefarious activities such as gambling, prostitution, and moving illegal goods like moonshine. In fact, they became known as "Shanghai Tunnels" because men were drugged, kidnapped and moved through the tunnels to sailing ships for labor, at least in the port cities. Today, these undergrounds are mostly tourist spots. Some supposedly are unsanctioned shelters for the homeless. And although rumors abound, it is doubtful Bend ever had such an intricate tunnel system.

Why not? Can you imagine digging tunnels through the lava rock?

That's not to say Bend doesn't make use of its basements and such, especially downtown. Obviously, most are used for storage, but we are seeing more and more underground spaces being converted into innovative places to hang out and make a profit.

I wrote about a few speakeasy-themed bars (The Cellar, Domaine Serene, and Cellar 65). We can also add The Capitol nightclub to the list. Sometimes this spot offers comedy nights, salsa lessons, and other fun stuff.

As a writer/bookworm, my favorite "underground" spot happens to be one of the most eclectic bookstores I've ever visited, the Underground Book Gallery. More than a typical bookstore, the

---

UNDERGROUND EXPLORATION

WHAT: Underground Bend and the Underground Book Gallery

WHERE: Downtown Bend

COST: Depends on which spot you visit!

PRO TIP: First Fridays of the month in downtown Bend are especially lively. During these you're guaranteed to find an exciting event in one of these underground spots.

144

The mural outside of the Underground Book Gallery (by Brandi Rowan)

shop is a cozy, creative space where local artisans and writers display and sell their wares. Besides unique art on the walls and a healthy selection of used books, UBG hosts events and artists featuring mixed media, sculptures, handmade clothing, and more. If you're lucky, you might even catch someone playing the piano or accordion!

Though Bend may not have a historic system of tunnels, our "underground" has tons of character and continues to grow and thrive.

When researching this question, it's surprising to discover how many cities in the US have (or had) hidden undergrounds. They were created for all types of purposes, ranging from catacombs to cold storage and everything in between!

OLDEST
IN CENTRAL OREGON

Is Prineville really the oldest settlement in Central Oregon?

Oregon became the 33rd state in 1859. Founded shortly afterward, in the 1870s, Prineville boasts the title of oldest settlement in Central Oregon!

The town claims a booming population of about 11,000. Steeped in tradition, as visitors walk along the downtown streets or drive slowly down Hwy. 27, Prineville seems a relaxed place where the old meets the new. A passerby would never suspect that a mega-corporation like Facebook exists right on the edges of town. Charming is perhaps too cliché a word, but Prineville exudes a simple, laid-back vibe not found in Bend, Redmond, or other rapidly growing cities in Oregon.

Though small and quiet, there is still much worth discovering in the town. The Crook County Courthouse, perhaps the most architecturally stunning in all of Oregon, sits imposingly on Third Street. Bowman Museum, once an old bank, carries a wealth of Crook County and Central Oregon history. Club Pioneer has been

War Paint *by Greg Congleton*

The oldest settlement in Oregon—in fact, in the entire Pacific Northwest—is Astoria, which was founded in 1811!

Left: *Mural by Katie Daisy and Karen Eland.*
Right: *Crook County Courthouse.*

PRINEVILLE, OREGON

WHAT: The oldest settlement in Central Oregon

WHERE: Prineville

COST: I guess it depends on what you do while visiting.

PRO TIP: Prineville is the unofficial rockhounding capital of the United States—and for good reason, as there are many sites nearby to find some cool rocks!

serving customers delicious food since World War II and pays tribute to the area's logging and cowboy roots throughout the restaurant. Murals are scattered around town, as are sculptures like the Wildland Firefighter Monument and *War Paint*. The Prineville Reservoir is a popular 3,000-acre recreational spot for swimming, boating, fishing, and camping. It also claims the rare designation of International Dark Sky Park, meaning it's an awesome place to stargaze!

Nearby, the Ochoco National Forest has tons of hiking and other outdoor opportunities, including a few obscure attractions included in this book. Prineville is definitely an escape from the hustle and bustle. Hopefully, it will stay that way.

SHADY BREWS

Are there any secret breweries?

In the deep forest of Deschutes River Woods, an eclectic neighborhood to the south of Bend, a hidden brewery awaits. Yep, this one is not on the famous Bend Ale Trail, and few people even know about its existence. Time to let out the secret!

Operating Shade Tree Brewing straight from his home, Larry Johnson takes the meaning of homebrewer to a whole new level. A bumpy drive down an unpaved county road leads to his property. Walk inside the large metal workshop and the first thing noticeable is either the shiny metallic brewing equipment or his pristine '66 Ford Mustang. Though Larry is an avid brewer, one look around tells you he is also a car aficionado. In fact, in his spare time he races in Madras!

Ask nicely and Larry will gladly give an in-depth tour of a building filled with kegs, bags of grains, hops, and every other piece of equipment and ingredient used in the brewing process. A large freezer stocks bottles of his signature bourbon barrel–aged Corvette Strong Ale and other experimental brews. Don't be surprised if he offers a taste (or a few) of his delicious concoctions. Bring a growler to fill up!

UNDISCOVERED BREWS

WHAT: Shade Tree Brewing

WHERE: Deschutes River Woods

COST: Prices vary

PRO TIP: Don't just show up at his place. Give him a call or text and schedule a time. Otherwise, you may have made a trip for nothing.

Larry and many other locals are a part of COHO (Central Oregon Homebrewers Association). Anyone interested in making (or drinking) beers, wines, meads, or other spirits can join!

Top: *Gary's Mustang.* Inset: *A tasty brew waiting to be opened*

It's not easy to do the brewing, marketing, and selling of your own product, but at times his beers are available at select locations around town. If you want a conversation about autos or alcohol, Larry's your guy. The care he takes in brewing is as meticulous as his prized Mustang, and true beer fans will appreciate his efforts.

OLDEST WATERING HOLE IN BEND

Where can I find Bend's oldest existing bar?

Bend's oldest watering hole sits quietly and unassumingly next to the green dinosaur managing the gas station on Galveston Avenue. Though perhaps not as well-known or popular as the multiple breweries nearby, the Westside Tavern (WST) has a much deeper history. Long before the plethora of breweries arrived in Central Oregon, the bartenders in this lava rock building were quenching the thirst of local patrons.

Sources differ, with some recording the tavern's origin as early as 1928. During Prohibition, the building became a mechanic shop for Model T Fords and later a bait and tackle shop for fishermen. Finally, in 1934, it returned to its true calling—as a local bar!

At the time Bend was a small town with around 15,000 enterprising citizens and growing quickly because the lumber mills were growing as well. The lumber employees stayed busy because the mills operated day and night. After shifts ended, the workers came to Westside at all hours to quench their thirst. Who wouldn't need a drink after that type of labor?

THE ETERNAL THIRST QUENCHER

WHAT: Westside Tavern

WHERE: 930 NW Galveston Ave.

COST: Depends on what you order!

PRO TIP: Local spots have a character all their own. Once you find a good one, stick to it.

The D&D Bar & Grill has been around a while as well. A mainstay since 1943, it's the "oldest" bar in downtown Bend!

To this day, WST is still mostly a locals' spot. A pool table, good music, good drinks, and a "let you know how they feel" staff make the place a no-nonsense favorite that has outlasted even the most popular bars over the years. The tavern has been through at least a few owners during its span, and though Bend is not known as a city with a vibrant nightlife, the Westside Tavern stays open later than most spots. In fact, it's often the place where bartenders from other establishments go after their shifts. You might find a tourist here and there, but locals keep this piece of history alive and thriving.

Westside Tavern on a cold, snowy day

BEWARE THE WITCHES!

Are those real witches paddling the Deschutes River in October?

Well, I won't be the one calling them witches, but judging by the way they are dressed, I would say it's quite possible they might cast some spells on those who chide them.

During the Witch Paddle held every Halloween, men and women decked out in the true garbs of sorcerers and enchantresses brave the Deschutes River in Bend. No matter the weather, these fearless souls glide through the chilly water on their paddleboards.

Supposedly, the event began in California when some friends dressed up as witches and got on the water one year to celebrate their birthdays, which all happened to fall on or near Halloween. Then, a woman from Portland who liked the idea started organizing the paddles on the Willamette River. At first, a dozen or so people paddled from Willamette Park to Tom McCall Waterfront Park. Quickly the event grew to several hundred participants and spread to other cities like Eugene and Bend.

PADDLING WITCHES

WHAT: The Witches of Bend

WHERE: Deschutes River

COST: Free to watch, bravery to participate!

PRO TIP: The bridge in the Old Mill District is a great spot to watch the event!

Its popularity continues to spread, and paddling covens are popping up as far away as the UK and Mexico!

Halloween seems to have overtaken Christmas with the number of activities and events available. If only we had time to participate in all of them!

These witches brave the cold of the Deschutes on Halloween.

In cities like Bend, the river gets mighty cold this time of year, so if these magic-loving witches cast a spell, it will most likely be to keep themselves warm or maintain balance on their boards. If nothing else, they look like they are having a blast!

TOP-SECRET INFORMATION

Why is there a flash drive stuck inside of a brick wall?

Shouldn't the question be, "What type of information is on this mysterious flash drive?" I mean, sure, cementing a flash drive into a brick wall is quite strange, but I am more concerned with what type of information it might hold—Deep, dark secrets about Bend? Classified files from the US government? Proof of an alien visit to Central Oregon?!

For those unaware or technologically challenged, flash drives are those tiny electronic devices that store or transfer information from your computers and such. We usually stick them into a USB (Universal Serial Bus) port to retrieve information. A brick wall is no USB, and one wonders why in the world it would be cemented into the side of a random building!

POSSIBLE ESPIONAGE?

WHAT: Hidden flash drive

WHERE: Downtown Bend

COST: Free, but I guarantee you'll spend some time searching.

PRO TIP: Do not attempt to pull the flash drive from the wall. These buildings are private property and as tempting as it may be, it's illegal.

The nearby downtown local businesses claim they have no idea how the flash drive got there. (Claim being the key word. They could be undercover agents as well.) Good luck trying to retrieve it

Reach out if you know how the flash drive ended up here. Are there more? It remains a mystery!

This flash drive may contain sensitive information.

from the cement. Even if that were possible, it would probably ruin the integrity of the data if it's not already corrupted from being out in the elements. This might be the single most difficult entry to locate in this book, thus top secret.

THE CURSED STONES

Will I be cursed if I take obsidian home?

Known as the coveted dragon glass in *Game of Thrones*, obsidian is a beautiful, volcanic, glass-like rock formed from molten lava that cools rapidly. Evidence of its use by humans goes back thousands of years, usually for jewelry or practical purposes like making arrowheads, blades, and other sharp weapons. Some believe it contains tremendous spiritual power.

After a trip to the Paulina Visitor Center people might think obsidian is cursed. Better yet, they will think twice about taking any home from the Big Obsidian Flow trail or the surrounding Newberry National Monument area. If the threat of paying a $500 fine or imprisonment doesn't scare visitors, the visitor center has a display of returned obsidian with notes to strike fear into the coldest of hearts. According to rangers, at least a few stones are returned every season. Along with them are accompanying notes with apologetic pleas such as, "Hey, we are truly sorry. We have had nothing but bad luck ever since we took this stone."

Obsidian is mostly used for ornamental purposes these days, but some believe it has positive cleansing and healing qualities. When bad luck arises, channel the negative energy into the stone, bury it, and allow Mother Earth to cleanse it. Keeping obsidian outside of the doors

Though you might be thinking twice about taking any obsidian home now, there are plenty of rockhounding spots in Oregon where removing the rock is perfectly legal. Glass Butte is a favorite.

*Obsidian stones found
on a rockhounding excursion*

and windows of a home is said to ward off evil.

Perhaps bad karma does befall those who take the rocks illegally, or maybe it's the hint of guilt that weighs upon them. No matter what your belief about the mysterious stone, it's best to leave it alone. Find it somewhere else to decorate your home or get rid of your bad juju.

SPIRITS IN THE ROCKS

WHAT: Obsidian stones

WHERE: Paulina Visitor Center

COST: Free to view the display, but taking rocks might incur a heavy fine!

PRO TIP: This is another spot that must be visited during the warmer months of the year. The visitor center is usually closed by November.

INDIGENOUS ATHLETES

What's the significance of the Girls & Boys Club Building?

Every town needs a recreational spot. Before Bend Parks & Recreation opened Juniper Fitness and Larkspur Community Center, the Bend Athletic Amateur Club & Gymnasium was the city's first such space. The noticeable red brick downtown, currently serving as the Boys & Girls Club, was once the heart of our community.

Strangely, before it opened to serve the public as an athletic club, it was utilized in 1918 as a hospital during the deadly influenza pandemic that struck the city. The following year the BAC finally opened for its true purpose as a venue to host graduations, dances, lectures, sporting events and more. Lucky members had access to amenities galore—a swimming pool, bowling alley, billiard room, steam baths, locker rooms, gymnasium, library, and a stage with enough seating for what was probably most of the population of Bend at the time!

Equally impressive, construction of the building was funded by community members and businesses. Three hundred thousand locally made bricks went into the original structure, no small feat. On the top corners perceptive observers may have noticed the intricate terra cotta carvings. These decorative cement pieces depict Indigenous athletes who look as if they are preparing for a race, a javelin throw, or some other competition. They definitely add to the structure's uniqueness.

Terra cotta carving of an Indigenous person

The building many years ago. Photo courtesy of Deschutes Historical Museum.

Ownership of the building later passed to the YMCA, then to the American Legion, and ultimately the Bend-La Pine School District until 1999. For the last 20-plus years it's been a place for kids to develop new skills, make lasting friendships, and have a great time. Sounds like it's always been a hub for community recreation!

A COMMUNITY REFUGE

WHAT: The Girls & Boys Club Building

WHERE: 500 NW St.

COST: Free to view

PRO TIP: The Boys & Girls Club plays a vital role in the Bend community. Consider volunteering or donating.

Currently, the Athletic Club of Bend is a members-only club with a wealth of amenities. Juniper Fitness and Larkspur Community Center, run by Bend Parks & Recreation, have everything you need.

SWIM, FISH, SWIM!

Where can I see fish without trying to catch them?

Central Oregon is blessed with beautiful, healthy rivers, many of which are world renowned for fishing, especially for trout. We have the Crooked, the Deschutes, the Metolius, the McKenzie, and several smaller rivers. Each has its own remarkable views and distinctive ecosystems.

Some folks don't care to go fishing but still love to see wildlife in action. They need travel no further than the Wizards Fish Hatchery. Near the cold, clear waters of the Metolius River, the hatchery serves as a place to incubate and rear rainbow trout and kokanee salmon. When the time comes, they are released into the local rivers for avid anglers to get their fill of recreational fishing. Other types of fish are also raised as part of the reintroduction program in the upper Deschutes Basin.

The hatchery makes a great trip for kids and adults. For only a quarter (yes, you are reading this correctly, a good old fashioned

FISH FRENZY

WHAT: Wizard Falls Fish Hatchery

WHERE: 7500 Forest Service Rd. 14, Camp Sherman

COST: Only 25 cents to feed the fish!

PRO TIP: Although a change machine is on site, stock up on quarters beforehand to feed the fish just in case!

Add the nearby Camp Sherman General Store to your list of stops. It first opened in 1918, and the old gas pumps outside and relics inside the store offer a veritable piece of history. The inside has a deli, fly shop, souvenirs, and about anything else you might need.

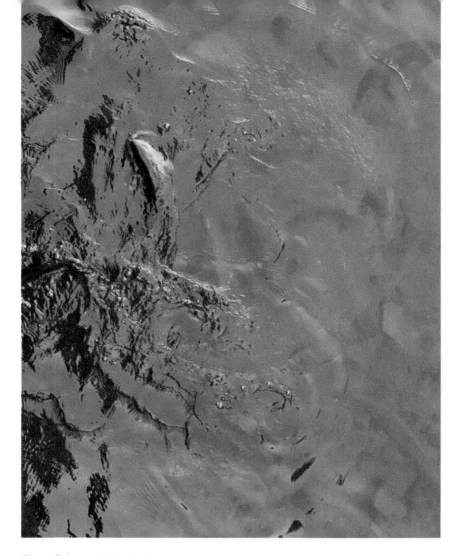

These fish want to be fed!

quarter), anyone can feed the fish in the pond or watch them swim wildly around in one of their many tanks.

While there, add the 6.2 mile loop trail along the banks of the Metolius to the bucket list, or at the very least take a walk around the pond, where you might see other wildlife. Plenty of campsites are nearby for those wanting to extend the experience.

One day, when my daughters move out of the house and I have the time, I plan to take up fly fishing. Until then, I'll appreciate my hikes with them along the river and feeding the fish for a quarter.

FOOD TRUCK HEAVEN

Why are there so many food trucks in Oregon?

Food trucks are nothing new to those of us who reside in Oregon. Here in Central Oregon, almost every town has their own food truck lots, with more individual carts popping up almost daily in the most random places.

We often take them for granted, but all these food choices often overwhelm visitors, because in many other places across the country the trucks are not as abundant. In fact, sources report that Portland has more food carts than any other city in the United States! Whether true or not, there is weight behind this statement.

So why are they so ubiquitous?

It all boils down to affordability and limited regulations. The cost of licenses and fees are significantly less than for a traditional brick and mortar restaurant. Local government regulations are minimal as long as health and safety requirements are met. And although food carts had been around in Oregon long before the 2007 recession, their popularity skyrocketed significantly afterwards.

A FOODIE UTOPIA

WHAT: Food trucks

WHERE: *All over* Central Oregon (and the entire state)

COST: Depends on what you want to eat!

PRO TIP: Try as many food trucks as you can!

Speaking of food, groups on social media sites will make you hungry every time you see a post! Check out the Chowhounds of Central Oregon and The Bend Foodie on Facebook to stay updated on new local food trucks, restaurants, and more!

The Podski Food Truck Lot

'The welcoming environment for food trucks is wonderful for food-loving entrepreneurs who want to open their own businesses and do what they enjoy, and they're wonderful for us because our taste buds have access to almost every type of food imaginable! If a specific type of food is not available, chances are good that it will be soon. It's no secret that we have so many food trucks, but now you have a better idea of why. Which one is your favorite?

BOB THE BEND ROCK

What's so special about a rock?

Meet Bend's newest adopted rock, Bob (Big Obvious Boulder). Never in all my years have I seen anything become so popular so quickly, especially a rock.

I mean, sure, Bob is handsome. I'd also say he's hard not to miss, but not so much. At 2 tons, this nice-sized lava rock makes no attempt to hide. In fact, he never moves. Yet, for some reason, like a magnet, he pulls automobiles toward him until BAM, there goes the paint job.

For almost a decade Bob has been in the same location of the retail complex near Franklin and Third Street, where the property manager originally had the intention of keeping drivers from

Bob, a friendly fella, just wanted to say hello to this vehicle.

running over the curb. Within a few months of his arrival, at least eight cars plowed into Bob. No harm done to the big guy, but the owners of the autos weren't too happy about the situation. Some local eateries felt so sorry for the drivers that they offered free food or a beverage. Would you go to that much trouble to get a free drink at the Pine Tavern? Not me!

Surprisingly, Bob quickly became a media sensation and now has a Facebook page with thousands of followers from all over the world. No, I'm serious. *All over the world.* It's quite silly (but fun) to scroll through the posts and see pictures of Bob's relatives (other accident-causing rocks). The sheer number of ridiculous posts is enough to give the most serious person a chuckle. Locals and tourists alike stop by to take pics and leave signs and such near Bob, proclaiming things like "The Undefeated Rock."

Hey, it is people's own business what they do with their time, and how the world found out about a rock in Bend, Oregon is a mystery. Still, any time we can turn misfortune into a positive thing is a win in my book. Thanks for bringing us all together, Bob!

BEWARE THE ROCK

WHAT: Bob the Bend Rock

WHERE: Franklin Avenue

COST: Free, unless you end up running into him

PRO TIP: Beware the magnetism of Bob!

No plans exist to move Bob at this point. In fact, he has become such a sensation that he may obtain some sort of protected monument status soon.

ULTIMATE SCAVENGER

I've learned so much about Central Oregon reading this book! Where can I keep learning?

We can never run out of news things to learn in life, which is the most exciting thing about the human experience in my opinion. Every country, state, city, and locale owns a unique history to be learned and experienced.

To get a crash course in the weird, wonderful, and obscure of Central Oregon, participate in an Ultimate Scavenger Hunt. Education through entertainment, these scavenger hunts blend an eclectic mixture of history and modern culture. Murals and sculptures, breweries, old buildings, food trucks, trails, sports, holes in the wall, strange oddities, creative local businesses . . . basically, everything unique and interesting about the area!

The most popular hunts are available year-round on well-known platforms such as Trip Advisor and Expedia. Larger hunts are held at least a few times a year, including the photo hunts, which are often geared more toward locals who already know the area (or at least think they do). During these spirited and competitive events, participants scour the city to find Bend's hidden treasures and win all sorts of prizes.

Hunts are not limited to Bend and can be done in Sisters, Redmond, and Prineville as well. Fair warning though: after participating in a few, you might become a Central Oregon savant

EDUCATIONAL ENTERTAINMENT

WHAT: Ultimate Scavenger Hunts

WHERE: Bend, Redmond, Sisters, Prineville, and beyond

COST: $20 and up

PRO TIP: For larger groups, break up into two groups (each with two to four people) and make the hunt a fun competition among friends.

All of these participants are having a blast finding clues on the Ultimate Scavenger Hunt! The clues are hidden in the envelope pictured at bottom right.

and be the envy of all your friends. At the very least, at the next party you'll have some great conversation starters about the area.

"Oh, by the way, did you know . . ."

How well do you know Bend and the rest of Central Oregon?

The Ultimate Scavenger personalizes hunts for businesses, holidays, special events, team building for kids, bachelorette parties, and more!

LOST LAKE

Is there really a lost lake in Central Oregon?

Actually, at least two Lost Lakes exist in Oregon. Why the first one is called "lost" remains a mystery. In fact, it's a well-known destination in the Mount Hood Wilderness with a popular resort. Visitors can camp in tents, yurts, or rent a cabin. The area has a boat launch, kayak and canoe rentals, and a general store. Again, not so lost and definitely not a secret.

The lesser known Lost Lake is not quite "lost" either. It is visible from Highway 20, or at least sometimes.

Then why do they call it lost?

Water from the lake drains into giant holes and seems to magically disappear!

When the snow melts on the mountains, the water rushes down from several streams and forms a body water large enough to kayak, paddleboard or take a dip. When it's full, usually in early spring, there are no sign of the holes, but you might see plenty of geese or other waterfowl. The lake is visible for a few months depending on the amount of snow and precipitation, but then . . . Gone!

Those giant holes are actually lava tubes formed thousands of years ago. The water empties in them and seeps through the layers of volcanic rock eventually becoming groundwater. By late summer the area is dry.

Oregon has over 1400 named lakes! Some of the unnamed and lesser known ones lie deep within the forests. For intrepid adventurers who want solitude and beauty, finding these lakes are often worth the trek.

A DISAPPEARING ACT

WHAT: Lost Lake

WHERE: Hwy. 20 near the summit of the Santiam Pass

COST: $5 Day Use, $12 for camping sites

PRO TIP: When using GPS, type in "Lost Lake Campground" and make sure you are NOT going to the one near Mount Hood!

Top and bottom left: Lost Lake in Spring
Right: One of the many streams flowing from the mountains to fill the lake

For curious spectators, late spring or early summer is your best bet to witness the spectacle. Otherwise, you get to see the full lake or a couple of large holes in the ground. Either way, the surrounding scenery is beautiful and fun to explore.

No need to plug the holes up. Let nature do her work. Besides, she is replenishing the water that we may end up drinking one day!

Beware the witches!

SOURCES

The Beginning: bendparksandrec. org/park/farewell-bend-park/; downtownbend.org/downtown-history.html#/.

A Volcano Here in the City?!: stateparks.oregon.gov/index. cfm?do=park.profile&parkId=33; kids.kiddle.co/Pilot_Butte_ (Oregon).

Quite the Character: oregonencyclopedia.org/articles/ klondike_kate/#.ZAD86nbMJPY.

A Phoenix from the Ashes: blog.mcmenamins.com/the-amazing-life-of-hugh-okane/; oregonencyclopedia.org/ articles/o_kane_building/#. ZAD9LHbMJPY.

Keepers of History: deschuteshistory.org/.

The McKay Cottage: dpls.overdrive. com/media/2665741; bendbulletin. com/localstate/mckay-had-a-large-role-in-bend-s-early-development/ article_087dd278-c386-57b3-8daf-ee67166f5eab.html; mckaycottage.com/.

Bend's Oldest Building: oregonencyclopedia.org/ articles/goodwillie_house/; en.wikipedia.org/wiki/ Goodwillie%E2%80%93Allen_ House; thecommonsbend.com/.

Smokestacks on the Horizon: oldmilldistrict.com/blog/history/ brooks-scanlon-mill-remnants-now-house-floral-arrangements/.

The Box Factory: boxfactorybend. com/history; deschuteshistory. org/saved-for-the-future-the-box-factory/#:~:text=Built%20in%20

1916%2C%20it%20was,did%20 the%20Box%20Factory%20 building.

The Lone Wood Building: en.wikipedia.org/wiki/N._P._ Smith_Pioneer_Hardware_Store; lonecrowbungalow.com/.

School on the River: waymarking. com/waymarks/wm89R_First_ Bend_School_Landmark.

Bend's Living Room: towertheatre. org/; oregonencyclopedia. org/articles/tower-theater/#. Y3EoE3bMJPY.

Railroad Battles: traveloregon. com/things-to-do/culture-history/ historic-sites-oregon-trail/arts-central-station/; curtdeatherage. wordpress.com/2019/04/13/ the-war-for-central-oregon/; historic-structures.com/or/bend/ bend_train_station.php.

Pilot Butte Inn: bendmagazine. com/pilot-butte-inn-history-bend/; torhanson. com/2017/03/27/the-finest-little-hotel-in-america-pilot-butte-inn/.

Secret Rooms: mcmenamins.com/ old-st-francis-school.

Yakaya: artinpublicplaces.org/ roundabout.html.

The Shire of Bend: bendbulletin. com/localstate/for-developers-of-bend-s-shire-dream-is-over/ article_25ee60a5-3d21-5d98-a3fd-46a7368aae2f.html; virtualglobetrotting.com/map/ the-shire-of-bend-oregon/view/ google/.

Glory Be to Bicycles!: webcyclery.
com/; bendfp.org/about-2/our-
roots/.

Beginning of the Brews:
deschutesbrewery.com/story/
about-us.html.

Homesteading Days: raprdblog.org/
our-work/2017/2/12/aj-tetherow-
home-saving-one-of-redmonds-
historic-treasures.

Bend Old Iron Works:
vintagemachinery.org/mfgindex/
detail.aspx?id=4721; bendsource.
com/culture/an-old-building-new-
idea-2430921.

One Flew Over the Cuckoo's Nest:
worthybrewing.com/.

Alley Art: visitbend.com/things-to-
do/art-museums-history/arts/tin-
pan-alley-art/.

Selfies with Celebrities:
bendsource.com/culture/a-
mix-tape-of-beloved-
musicians-15752013;
silvermoonbrewing.com/.

**Fujioka, the Japanese Sister City
of Bend:** fujiokatown.web.fc2.
com/Bend/Bend-Fujioka.htm;
en.wikipedia.org/wiki/Fujioka,_
Gunma.

The High Desert Museum:
highdesertmuseum.org/.

Stylish Statues: artinpublicplaces.
org/roundabout.html.

Reliving the Oregon Trail: blm.gov/
visit/huntington-wagon-road;
oregontic.com/oregon-heritage-
trees/huntington-wagon-road-
junipers/.

Lava Bears: en.wikipedia.org/wiki/
Lava_bear.

A Rainbow of Bottles: Interview
with shop owner Jacqueline
Smith; foundnaturalgoods.com/.

Bear Hugs and Beer: Interview
with Lauren Redman;
newportavemarket.com/.

The Last Blockbuster:
bendblockbuster.com/.

Bird Watching at Its Best:
ebird.org/hotspot/
L447435?yr=all&m=&rank=hc;
centraloregondaily.
com/%E2%96%B6%EF%B8%8F-
the-great-outdoors-bird-
watching-at-the-hatfield-lakes/.

A Layover at the Caves: blm.gov/
visit/redmond-caves-recreation-
site.

The Dry Canyon: outdoorproject.
com/united-states/oregon/
redmonds-dry-canyon.

The Surviving Homestead:
bendparksandrec.org/park/riley-
ranch-nature-reserve/.

**Smith Rock, Hollywood
Superstar:** stateparks.oregon.
gov/index.cfm?do=park.
profile&parkId=36; imdb.com/
search/title/?locations=smith%20
rock%20state%20park,%20
oregon,%20usa.

A Rock Garden:
petersenrockgarden.org/;
oregonencyclopedia.org/
articles/petersen-rock-garden/#.
ZAD733bMJPY.

Old-School Movie Theaters:
sistersmoviehouse.
com/; tinpantheater.com/;
mcmenamins.com/old-st-francis-
school/old-st-francis-theater;
odemtheaterpub.com/.

A Cowboy Dinner:
cowboydinnertree.com/.

The Old Man: stateparks.oregon. gov/index.cfm?do=park. profile&parkId=32; outdoorproject.com/united-states/oregon/big-tree-ponderosa-pine.

Western Style Town: sisterscountry. com/live-here/sisters-history#!directory; nuggetnews. com/story/2021/04/06/news/ sisters-a-history-of-pioneer-resilience/31833.html.

World War II Camp: sunriverresort. com/blog/sunriver-resorts-historic-great-hall/; bendbulletin. com/localstate/sunriver-great-hall-was-part-of-army-training-exercise/article_29671b78-8cdd-5063-ac1c-387944803741.html; oregonencyclopedia.org/articles/ camp_abbot/#.ZAD8tHbMJPY.

Stargazing: worthyenvironmental. org/hopservatory; darksky.org/ news/prineville-reservoir-state-park-announcement/; snco.org; pmo.uoregon.edu/.

Snow and Climate: usclimatedata. com/climate/bend/oregon/united-states/usor0031.

The Mighty Pillar: fs.usda. gov/recarea/ochoco/ recarea/?recid=38758; Ontko, Gale. Thunder Over the Ochocos: The Gathering Storm. Vol. 1, Maverick, 1993.

I Ain't Afraid of No Ghosts: bendsource.com/news/ ghost-towns-of-central-oregon-14722697; sos.oregon. gov/archives/exhibits/ghost/ Pages/transportation-shaniko. aspx; photographoregon. com/Millican-Oregon.html; visitoregon.com/oregon-ghost-towns/#:~:text=Another%20 great%20ghost%20town%20 is,of%20a%20time%20gone%20 by.

A Unique Cemetery: oregonencyclopedia.org/ articles/camp_polk_and_ camp_polk_meadows_ preserve/#.ZAD7jXbMJPY; oregonencyclopedia.org/articles/ camp_polk_cemetery/#.ZAD6-HbMJPZ.

Haircuts and Belt Buckles: lkbarbershopbend.com/.

Astronaut Training: opb.org/ pressroom/article/new-opb-documentary-explores-moon-country-in-central-oregon-a-once-unique-training-ground-for-nasa-astronauts/#:~:text=Astronauts%20 visited%20Hole%20in%20 the,flows%20and%20 studied%20the%20terrain; oregonencyclopedia.org/articles/ newberry_national_volcanic_ monument/#.ZAD8aHbMJPY

This Land Is Your Land, This Land Is My Land: oregonhistoryproject. org/narratives/this-land-oregon/ people-politics-and-environment-since-1945/oregons-public-lands/

Dee Wright Observatory: fs.us-da.gov/recarea/willamette/ recarea/?recid=4403: tha-toregonlife.com/2018/08/ dee-wright-observatory/?fbclid=I-wAR3VMEc_XSFSK7QWpUT9x-oRc5Qabnmm0ucDwic4lXdVd-9vXek_7aiT8PK8Y

Indigenous People: warmsprings-nsn.gov/; critfc.org/ member-tribes-overview/ the-confederated-tribes-of-the-warm-springs-reservation-of-oregon/#:~:text=A%20 640%2C000%2Dacre%20 reservation%20 in,(Dock%2Dspus)%20bands.

Cold, Cool Caves: ohdgrotto.caves.org/caves/caves-of-central-oregon.

Attention All Pilots!: airnav.com/airport/8OR5.

Whole in the Wall: mitchelloregon.us/; atlasobscura.com/places/mitchell-shoe-tree.

Water Is Life: headwaterseconomics.org/wp-content/uploads/Deschutes_River_Basin_Agricultural_Report.pdf; en.wikipedia.org/wiki/Deschutes_River.

Illegal but Fun!: gompersdistillery.com/; backsidekegs.com/.

Rejuvenating Hot Springs: breitenbush.com/; cranehotsprings.com/; summerlakehotsprings.com/; belknaphotsprings.com/; fs.usda.gov/recarea/willamette/recarea/?recid=4391.

What's Up, Gnomie?: thelittlewoody.com/.

Watch Out for the Fire!: oregonlookouts.weebly.com/bend-awbrey-butte.html; google.com/maps/d/u/0/viewer?mid=1xd2ad3Cg5-3Mxc7gKthLNsrlaVo&femb=1&ll=43.7371632969919%2C-121.60404795&z=7.

Little Rangers: fs.usda.gov/detail/deschutes/news-events/?cid=STELPRDB5423161; nps.gov/crla/learn/kidsyouth/beajuniorranger.htm.

Quilts, Quilts, and More Quilts!: soqs.org/contests.

Balancing Rocks: atlasobscura.com/places/metolius-balancing-rocks.

Christmas Tree, O Christmas Tree: recreation.gov/tree-permits/b8d732af-ec55-11ea-b83f-6e0e43d29f74#:~:text=and%20tree%20height.-,Where%20to%20Cut%20Your%20Tree,slopes%20facing%20north%20or%20east.

Digging for Fossils: nps.gov/joda/index.htm; oregonpaleolandscenter.com/wheeler-high-school-fossil-beds.

Haunted Bend: deschuteshistory.org/events/2023-historical-haunts-of-downtown-bend-walking-tours-2/.

Mining for Gold!: fs.usda.gov/recarea/ochoco/recreation/hiking/recarea/?recid=38756&actid=50; prinevillechamber.com/things_to_do/ochoco-mines/#:~:text=Hidden%20all%20over%20the%20Ochocos,Lode%20Mine%20and%20Independent%20Mine.

Easy Trails: hdffa.org/wp-content/uploads/2023/06/2023-high-desert-food-trail-brochure-web.pdf.

Underground Bend: instagram.com/undergroundbookgallery/.

Oldest in Central Oregon: oregonencyclopedia.org/articles/prineville/; raprdblog.org/our-work/2017/2/12/aj-tetherow-home-saving-one-of-redmonds-historic-treasures.

Shady Brews: Interview with Larry Johnson; shadetreebrewing.com/.

Oldest Watering Hole in Bend: bendsource.com/special-issues-and-guides/go-old-school-5643126.

Beware the Witches!: oregonlive.com/life-and-culture/erry-

2018/10/a6e688dc885752/
hundreds-of-witches-pick-paddl.
html#:~:text=The%20witch%20
paddle%20on%20the,dozen%20
participants%20to%20
several%20hundred.

Top-Secret Information: Interview with various business owners.

The Cursed Stones: Interview with friendly park ranger; fs.usda.gov/recarea/deschutes/recarea/?recid=38458&ac-tid=119s.

Indigenous Athletes: https://npgallery.nps.gov/GetAsset/29c91fdd-b931-4830-b9f0-f38a2dcdfa39; oregonencyclopedia.org/articles/bend_amateur_athletic_club_gymnasium/.

Swim, Fish, Swim!: https://myodfw.com/wizard-falls-hatchery-visitors-guide; bendbulletin.com/business/camp-sherman-store-a-hub-of-activity-in-a-peaceful-central-oregon-paradise/article_fea59166-808a-11ed-9a79-373c87792a61.html.

Food Truck Heaven: https://j460oregonbrands.uoregon.edu/2015/02/10/why-food-carts/

Bob the Bend Rock: facebook.com/groups/695492805841135.

Ultimate Scavenger: https://livelocalbend.com/business/ultimate-scavenger/; tripadvisor.com/Attraction_Review-g51766-d17559449-Reviews-Ultimate_Scavenger-Bend_Central_Oregon_Oregon.html.

Lost Lake: fs.usda.gov/recarea/willamette/recarea/?recid=13362; livescience.com/50749-lost-lake-lava-tube.html#:~:text=It%20likely%20falls%20down%20the,they%20escaped%20into%20the%20atmosphere.

Fire Lookout

The Little Woody Barrel-Aged Beer, Cider & Whiskey Festival
Photo courtesy of Lay It Out Events

INDEX